2500 Miles on the
COASTAL STEAMER

Written and edited by:
Erling Welle-Strand

Published by
Troms County Steamship Company, Tromsø
Vesteraalen Steamship Company, Stokmarknes
Nordenfjeldske Steamship Company, Trondheim
Ofoten Steamship Company, Narvik
and Norway Travel Association
(Nortrabooks)

Photographers: Aune Foto page 16–17, 25, 73, 80, Johan Berge 9, 20, 33, 72, 77, 96, Terje Gustavsen 53, Husmo Foto 21, 29, 37, 40, 49, 52, 56, 57, 61, 64, 65, 84, 85, Bjørn Jacobsen 69, Røstad Foto 13, 38, Helge Sunde 41, To-Foto 44, Erling Welle-Strand 28, 32, 36, 45, 48, 60, 76, 81, 93. Cover photo: Aune Foto.
English translation by Christopher Norman.
Printed in Norway 1984 by A.s John Grieg, Bergen
Sixteenth Impression
ISBN 82-90103-07-7

CONTENTS:

The companies operate the following coastal steamers:

TROMS COUNTY STEAMSHIP COMPANY

M.s «Nordstjernen»	M.s «Nordlys»
M.s «Polarlys»	M.s «Midnatsol»

VESTERAALEN STEAMSHIP COMPANY

M.s «Finnmarken»	M.s «Kong Olav»
	M.s «Lofoten»

NORDENFJELDSKE STEAMSHIP COMPANY

M.s «Harald Jarl»	M.s «Ragnvald Jarl»

OFOTEN STEAMSHIP COMPANY

M.s «Nordnorge»	M.s «Narvik»

The Coastal steamer

The journey by coastal steamer from Bergen to Kirkenes is an unforgettable trip covering a distance of over 1 200 miles, i.e. equivalent to round the entire west coast of Alaska as far as the Bering Straits, and penetrating just as far north. It runs along a coastline which has no equal in Europe, past eight of Norway's counties, with a coastal population of over half a million souls, living in towns and villages from Bergen in the South to Kirkenes in the North. A unique feature of this journey is that half of it lies north of the Arctic Circle. In other regions of the earth the land that lies north of the Arctic Circle is barren and forbidding, but thanks to the soothing influence of the Gulf Steam the inhabitants of Norway have been able to extend the outposts of Western civilization over 500 miles into what would otherwise have been a land of eternal ice and snow. No visitor to the Land of the Midnight Sun fails to be impressed with the luxuriance of the vegetation. En route we pass the westernmost point of Norway, which lies just outside the Sognefjord, the northernmost (at North Cape), and the most easterly, just to the east of Vardø.

Those who make this trip will understand how important the coastal steamer is to the population who live in the northernmost part of Norway, and what enterprise, experience and seamanship were necessary to establish this link and maintain it. It is now more than 90 years since the first coastal steamer, the S.S. *Vesteraalen*, sailed out from Trondheim with Richard With, the pioneer of this route, on her bridge. From that day the coastal steamer has run day and night, summer and winter. The arrival of the first coastal steamer was celebrated like a national holiday all the way up the coast, and the 2nd of July, 1893, was for many years thereafter refferred to as the national day of North Norway. Before that date the coastal steamer only operated during the summer months, and docked at night.

Today coastal steamers operate both ways all the year round. Four shipping lines — the Troms, the Nordenfjeldske, Vesteraalens, and the Ofoten Steamship Company — co-operate to maintain this line with 11 coastal express steamers, sturdy passenger ships which also take a certain amount of cargo. These 11 vessels run between Bergen and Kirkenes and cover an annual aggregate of close on a million miles, or a distance equal to 36 times round the earth at the equator.

The further north we get, the greater the importance of the coast express to the daily lives of the inhabitants. The arrival of the coastal steamer is still *the* event of the day in some ports of call; people come crowding down on to the quay, young and old having learnt to recognise the boat by its siren.

Passengers on board the steamer and the people on the quay appraise one another with mutual curiosity. Soon the winches are rumbling; cargo is landed, and new bales taken on board. Every little port of call has its own personality, and the further north one goes during the summer months, the less distinction do people make between day and night. It is common to see people taking their "afternoon stroll" between 1 and 2 o'clock in the morning.

The passengers on board constitute a community of their own, and represent every stratum of society in Norway, to which are added in the summer months tourists from all over the world.

Watched from the coastal steamer the scene is continually changing, and there is always something new to see from the rail or from your deck-chair, where you feel the faint throb of the engine beating out its muffled tattoo. There is tense expectation in the air when the rhythmical sound of the engine suddenly dies down and the steamer glides noiselessly through the water towards the quay, where the teeming crowd waits.

The Midnight Sun gives the summer night its own special blend of daylight, with infinite shades and nuances according to the vagaries of wind and weather. In the extreme north it is not only Thomas Carlyle who has been deeply moved by the cliffs of grey-green granite and the ocean heaving slowly to the Arctic swell, with the sun just above the horizon, glowing with the fitful light of a guttering candle.

In the spring some of the small islands are white with the flower of the cloud-berry, as after a fall of snow: in the autumn they glow red and gold with the ripe fruit.

In the depth of winter, when the only daylight in Troms is a short transition from a roseate dawn to a deep blue twilight, the coastal steamer ploughing north experiences the dramatic opposite of the Midnight Sun—the dazzling firework display of the Northern Lights—when the sky flames in a myriad hues and the darkness is stabbed with beams of light. Among the many attractions of the trip by coastal steamer in winter is the unforgettable sight of the Lofoten fisheries, which take place in January—April, with thousands of fishermen engaged, and a forest of masts tightly packed in an area of a few square miles off the rocky Lofoten islands.

In the county of Troms nature reveals her most exuberant side as a contrast to the bleak and barren wastes of Finnmark. In Troms the coastal steamer threads its way through narrow sounds and fjords, often rounding a corner to come, with startling suddenness, to its port of call.

The stretch from the Polar Circle up to East Finnmark is remarkable for the colonies of birds which live on countless rocks and cliffs. Here a variety of birds nest in their millions—the quarrelsome guillemot, the arrogant oyster-catcher, the sociable kiddow, puffins, eider-duck and comorants, all tenanting rocks which are literally chalky with bird-droppings.

More than any other form of transport the coastal steamer claims you for its own, and at all times offers sights and sounds and experiences that are for ever new and fascinating. It becomes your moving home, speedy enough to present you with constantly changing panorama, but not too swift to prevent you savouring to the full each hour of the live-long day, or to reflect and rest. Impressions have time to mature and mellow into memory.

FIRST DAY:

Leaving Bergen

The steamer sets a course down the fjord, and our long journey to
the north has started.

*

Bergen Astern lies the town of *Bergen*, a town no longer confined by the
encircling mountains, but spreading up the pine-clad slopes. The
colourful buildings contrast effectively with the forbidding
mountain tops which stand sentinel around, and contrast is one of
Bergen's greatest charms—contrast between the forbidding
mountains and the welcoming sea, between new and old, and even
in the mixture of solid bourgeois virtues and devil-may-care
attitude which is typical of the inhabitants. These delightful
contrasts place the old Hanseatic city among the towns one seldom
forgets.

The original town occupied a relatively small site, but as more
and more people moved out to the surrounding municipalities, four
of these were in 1972 merged with Bergen. This had once been
known as the town set between seven hills, but it would be more
correct now to talk of the town between seven fjords. Today it has a
population of some 210 000, which makes it Norway's second
largest town. The harbour is the natural centre of a town whose
main interests are commerce and sea-faring, and around Vågen we
find the oldest houses. On the east side stands Bergenhus castle,
Norway's most cherished relic from medieval times. Just beyond is
another cultural treasure—the quay with the old merchants'
houses. The wooden houses and narrow streets of Nordnes on the
other side of Vågen, too, speak to us of times long past. The centre
of the town was rebuilt after a fire in 1916, but the shops and
business premises here blend harmoniously with the rest of the
town. A new Bergen has sprung up along the fjord to the north and
at the foot of the mountains to the south and east.

Founded by King Olav Kyrre (the Peaceful) in 1070, Bergen is
one of Norway's oldest towns. In the 12th and 13th centuries, when
Norway was at the peak of her power, and there was lively
intercourse between the mother country and the Norwegian
colonies in the islands to the west, Bergen was Norway's capital.
Here the Norwegian kings had their residence, and many scenes of
magnificent pomp were witnessed in this port, which at that time
had no less than 13 churches and 15 abbeys. One of the most
colorful events of his age was the coronation of King Håkonsson by
Cardinal de Sabina, an event which maybe marked a climax in the
history of medieval Norway.

8

"Hail to thee, Bergen, fair centre of trade, Stretching thy arms o'er the sail-studded sea."

Bergen owed wealth and prominence to the fish export trade. The town was the collecting point of one of the most important products in the Middle Ages—dried fish—which the men of North Norway brought to Bergen every spring and autumn in their boats, and which local and foreign merchants then shipped to the new towns that were growing up along the shores of the North Sea and the Baltic. Gradually the Hanseatic League acquired a monopoly of foreign trade, and the Norwegian Crown became more and more dependent on the land-owning classes of East Norway. Eventually the monarchy moved its residence to Oslo, but throughout the

Middle Ages Bergen remained Scandinavia's largest and most important trade centre, and far into the 19th century it was Norway's largest town.

Shortly after the middle of the 16th century the power of the Hanseatic League declined. Norwegian merchants were competing afresh with their foreign rivals, and enterprising merchants and craftsmen from Holland, North Germany, England and Scotland settled in large numbers in Bergen, which at all times has sought impulses from the outside world. A new period of prosperity was ushered in, an age which in the cultural sphere produced Scandinavia's first and greatest writer of comedies, Ludvig Holberg. Bergen continued to prosper in the 19th and 20th centuries. There was a tremendous expansion in shipping and Bergen was for many years Norway's leading shipping town. Prosperity brought added capital to the town, and industries grew apace. The arts, too, throve in the cosmopolitan atmosphere, and produced many figures of world renown, such as J. C. Dahl, the father of modern Norwegian painting, Ole Bull, who laid the Old and the New World at his feet with his magic fiddle, and above all Bergen's greatest son, Edvard Grieg, who in undying tones portrayed his country and his people. In honour of Grieg International Music Festivals are held annually in the first fortnight of June.

The oldest building in Bergen is the Church of St. Mary (Mariakirken), built in the first half of the 12th century, one of the most beautiful Norman churches in Norway, with richly decorated portals and a beautiful altar screen. The castle of Bergenhus goes back to the 13th century. Håkon's Hall, in this castle, was part of the royal manor, and was used as a banqueting hall on State occasions. The Rosenkrantz Tower was erected round a fortress tower from the time of King Håkon Håkonsson, the old tower being incorporated in the new and more impressive building. The new tower not only formed part of the town defences, but was also the residence of the local governor. There are also a number of other historical buildings in Bergenhus castle, which has undergone extensive repairs following the explosion that rocked Bergen harbour in 1944.

In one of the old merchants' houses on the quay a Hanseatic Museum, which is a true copy of the house of a Lübeck merchant, has been installed. Schøtstuene, the picturesque buildings used by local merchants from Hanseatic days and right up to about 1840, can still be seen opposite the Church of St. Mary (Mariakirken). Bryggens Museum exhibits medieval finds from extensive excavations.

In Bergen we find Norway's first College of Business Administration, Norway's second University, and the Christian Michelsen

10

Research Institute. Bergen University has valuable natural history collections, as well as archaeological and art sections. Probably of greater interest to the visitor is the Fisheries Museum, which with admirable clarity presents the development of Norwegian fisheries. The Bergen Art Gallery, the Stenersen's Collection and the Rasmus Meyer Collection at Lake Lungegårdsvann contain valuable Norwegian and European paintings. Of special interest at the Museum of Arts and Crafts are antique Bergen silver and Chinese collections.

As town planning replaces the old with the new, much of Bergen's past is inevitably being demolished. Fortunately a selection of some of the finest and most interesting buildings in Bergen have been moved piecemeal to a special part of town, Old Bergen, in Sandviken. The Aquarium in Bergen boasts the largest collection of salt-water fish and marine animals in Europe, as well as a complete "set" of Norwegian fresh-water fish. In the outskirts of Bergen, close to the charming little Nordåsvann Lake, lies "Troldhaugen", the home of Edvard and Nina Grieg. Close to the water's edge stands the famous pavilion where the composer used to work. On the way to "Troldhaugen" a visit should be paid to Fantoft Stave Church.

The local economy, like the citizens, is "a mixed bag". Shipping and export of fish, traditional sources of livelihood, are still important. But with thousand industrial and business enterprises of various kinds, growing commitment to the off-shore oil industry in the North Sea, over two thousand shops, wide-ranging wholesale trade, banking and insurance, not to forget public services, Bergen has a great many legs to stand on. Industry and construction, trade and shipping, administrative and service activities, each account for one third of all employed persons. So it's a moot point whether the old tag from the Bergen hymn fits any longer. It runs more or less as follows:

Hail to thee Bergen, fair centre of trade,
Stretching thy arms o'er the sail-studded sea.

Finally no visitor should leave Bergen without having climbed one of the seven mountain tops so as to enjoy a bird's eye view of this remarkable and beautiful town. The cable railway, running to the top of Fløien, over a thousand feet above sea level, is the most convenient way to do this.

The stretch Bergen-Måløy is described under day 12.

2nd DAY:

Måløy to Kristiansund N

During the night our trusty ship has steamed steadily through the archipelago and made an early morning call at Florø.

Now she noses her way through the narrow Skatestraumen, where the tide may run up to six knots, and passes close to **Hornelen** *Hornelen,* a mighty rock that rises sheer 860 m from the sea. Legend has it that King Olav Trygvesson rescued one of his men who had got stuck climbing up, and that the king himself later scaled this impressive peak. Be that as it may, the feat was performed in 1897 by Kristen Bing, a Bergen lawyer. Take a good look, and you'll discover a "profile" of Queen Victoria on a projection just below the summit, as well as a large cleft. This gets bigger every year, and ships are now forbidden to sound their sirens, in case this start a landslide. On this remarkable mountain witches are said to have foregathered on Midsummer's Night. From here they could look down on Vingen on the mainland with its rock carvings, 2000 in all, mainly depicting deer, comprising the biggest collection in the North.

Måløy *Måløy* is an important fishing centre, where large quantities of fish, dogfish and skate and other species, are landed. The North Sea and its ample resources are garnered by local trawlers, who deliver their catches to refrigerator and filleting plant, klip-fish drying yards, and canning and herring oil factories. The growth of the fishing industry has given Måløy a leading position as an exporter of fresh fish. Måløy will be remembered as the target of an Allied commando raid in December 1941, which caught the Germans unawares and resulted in violent street fighting and the destruction of vital installations. A 1,224-metre-long bridge, opened in 1974, has linked Måløy to the mainland. When the wind is blowing from a particular quarter the bridge "sings" a high C, loud enough to keep people awake.

After negotiating the Ulvesund (Wolf Sound) our ship shapes a course for Stad, and as we come abeam of Skongsnes Light we catch **Selje** sight of the island of *Selje* off the coast of Stadland.

Here, so legend relates, the beautiful Irish princess Sunniva fled from her pagan suitor and took refuge in a cave. People on the mainland warned Earl Håkon, but when he set out to capture the Irish fugitives, a stone fell down from the mountain side, blocking the entrace to the cave. Sunniva and her followers perished, and later on signs and lights could be observed above Selje. Olav Trygvesson, who introduced Christianity to Norway from abroad, had a church built on the island, and St. Sunniva soon became the patron saint of West Norway.

12

Hornelen rises 860 m sheer out of the sea. According to legend King Olav Trygvesson climbed the precipitous east wall. Be that as it may, it was scaled by Kristian Bing and Anders Jeremiassen in 1897.

The ruins of a Benedictine Abbey are still to be found at Selje. The stones were in the past often used as ballast by the traders who sailed from Bergen to North Norway. They would often take a few stones on board while they were waiting for good weather at Selje, before sailing across the open sea at Stad. Sic transit gloria mundi.

In clear weather we should be able to see as far as the Ålfot glacier to the south-east before we pass Hovdetjøtta, where the sea has drilled weird tunnels into the rock. Between Hovden and *Kjerringa*, the 1800 ft. cliff that defies the ocean, like a clenched fist,

13

and marks the outermost point of Stadland we look straight into Ervik with its St. Swithin's chapel, erected in memory of the costal express that foundered south of Hovdan, after being hit by Allied bombs in 1943, with the loss of 40 lives. On the sandy beach at Ervika many strange objects have been dug up, from Roman bronze buckles to Anglo-Saxon silver coins, in years when the wind has blown away more sand than the sea managed to pile up. Throughout history many proud vessels have been wrecked off Stad: in fact this stretch of sea—Stadhavet—is considered one of the toughest along this coast. Among seafaring men Stad has an evil reputation going back to Saga times. There are many accounts—not least foreign—of ships wrecked off Stad. In 1594 15 Nordland sloops went down here with the loss of some 30–40 lives. It is hardly surprising that many fishermen preferred to haul their open boats across the Dragseid isthmus in order to avoid this perilous stretch of sea. Locals still remember fishing smacks being pulled on runners across the cobbled road. Now, incidentally, we are leaving the North Sea and are entering on the Norwegian Sea.

The leads to Ålesund run through the Flåvær archipelago and the Røyrasund narrows. On the left lies the fishing village of Eggesbønes, and on the right the large herring-oil factory at Moltustrand. Between Gurskøy and Bergsøy we pass under the 543-metre-long Herøy Bridge and note that all the inhabited islands **Torvik** in Herøy are linked with lofty bridges. Further on we call at *Torvik,* and opposite Torvik, on Hareidland, we should make out Ulsteinvik, famous for its football team and shipbuilding yards. As we round the point and make our way up Breisund, we shall see, due **Runde** west, the *Runde* birdrock, the most southerly of its kind in Norway and the home of some half-a-million sea birds, comprising at least 32 different species. Numerically the kittywake, dominates with 300,000 inhabitants, followed by the puffin, mustering some 40,000, while minority groups include such rarities as the gannet and the arctic petrel. Runde too can now be reached by road, via tunnel, embankments and a 432-metre-long bridge.

Ålesund *Ålesund* (pop. 35,000) is built on three islands, and is named after the narrow sound which runs between two of them, Nørvøy and Aspøy, where the core of the town stands.

Ålesund is a young town—celebrated its centenary in 1948 — but its roots are old. Three miles east of the town lies the old medieval market town of Borgund, which fell into a decline when the Hanseatic League acquired its trade monopoly. Ålesund was practically entirely rebuilt after a great fire in 1904 had destroyed most of the buildings. It took only 3 years to re-erect the town, which gave it a singularly uniform Jugend style look. Some of these have been pulled down and replaced, but the majority have remained. Old houses are now being modernized, but the exterior remains unchanged. Thus few town have, like Ålesund, retained their appearance in our century.

Ålesund is Norway's largest fishing port, the home of a large oceangoing fleet operating all the year round, catching halibut in Baffin Bay, Greenland shark in the Straits of Greenland, herring off the coast of Iceland, ling in the North Sea, cod and capelan along the Norwegian coast, and whales in the Norwegian Sea. From an early age Ålesund specialized in Arctic expeditions, and a number of sealers are equipped and sent out every year, especially to the waters between Greenland and Canada.

Only 400–500 hands are required to man Ålesund's modern and efficient fishing fleet. Thousands of people are employed on shore in fish processing, refrigerator and deep-freeze plants, train oil refineries, canning and smoking factories, etc., and in the export of fish products. The fishing industry also provides work for local shipbuilding yards specialising in fishing vessels, repair yards and various other service enterprises connected with fishing. In fact, for every member of a seagoing boat there are nearly ten persons employed ashore. To complete the picture of the local economy we should mention knitwear and clothing, plastics and furniture, as well as one of Scandinavia's largest cheese and butter export dairies.

From Aksla, the "local" mountain, 625 ft. above the streets below, there is a view which even surpasses the panorama from Fløien in Bergen. Not only is there a fascinating bird's eye view of the town, but also a view of the myriad islands and soaring peaks of the Sunnmøre Alps. It can be reached by taxi, or by climbing 418 steps from the town park. In the park stands a statue of Gange Rolf, a gift from the town of Rouen in France. The sagas relate that Gange Rolf was the son of the great Ragnvald, Earl of Møre, traditionally regarded as the first ruler of the Orkneys. The son, like the father a mighty Viking, turned his face to more southerly climes, and history relates that a certain Rollon was in 911 made feudal lord of Normandy by Charles the Simple. In the park there is also a statue to the memory of William II, the German Kaiser, who came to the assistance of the town after the great fire of 1904. Other local attractions include the local museum with its Arctic section and the fishery collection with its many quaint old boats, Ålesund Aquarium containing all the species native to the North Sea and the Norwegian Sea, and Ålesund Church with its frescoes and stained glass.

Between Godøy and Valderøy, immediately to the west of Ålesund, lies the island of *Giske*. In the Middle Ages this was the **Giske** seat of the powerful Giske family. Tora of Giske married Harald

15

From any point in Molde the famous panorama can be seen, comprising 87 snow-

with the Romsdal mountains providing a majestic backdrop.

Hårdråde, and bore him two sons, Magnus and Olav Kyrre, who both became kings. At one time the Giske family owned 126 farms in Sunnmøre, 75 in Romsdal, and 13 in North Norway, but their wealth and power were not only based on landed property, for they were also engaged in fishing and commerce. Giske Church, which is faced in pale marble, was once the family chapel. On the west side of Valderøy can be seen one of the most fascinating caves in Sunnmøre, hollowed out by the constant action of the sea during the inter-glacial period. Finds have shown that the 130-yard-deep cave was inhabited during the Stone Age. Valderøy is linked by bridge to Vigra, on which Ålesund airport is situated, as well as a radio station and the Blindshaugen burial grounds with their late Roman graves. Blindheim was the seat of the local ruling family of that name in the 12th century.

To the south the Sunnmøre Alps come into view. Most prominent among the peaks is Jønshorn (4,750 ft.), rising sheer up from the Hjørundfjord and the monarch of the Sunnmøre range, the Kolåstind Peak (4,800 ft.), first climbed in 1876 by the famous English mountaineer Slingsby.

Gliding across Lepsøyrevet, where Norway's first lightship was placed in 1857, we turn up the Molde Fjord. On our right lies Brattvåg, a busy little urban community, which owes its growth during the last generations to local initiative and enterprise. The factory at Brattvåg has an international reputation as the manufacturer of deck machinery. Steaming along the low forest-clad shore of Tautra, we head for Molde.

Molde Protected against northerly and westerly winds, *Molde* lies at the foot of the hills, facing a fjord which opens out on to a magnificent panorama of 87 snow-capped peaks, a panorama which has made the town famous all over the world. Molde has been called "the Town of Roses". Though the profusion of roses may not impress all travellers, the fact remains that a great many plants which really belong to far warmer climes grow here on sheltered slopes.

The town of Molde (population to-day approximately 21,000) was founded in 1742, but developed little until recent times, as it lay too far from the sea to compete in the fishing industry. On the other hand it was conveniently situated for trade with the coastal and fjord villages, and it was in commerce as well as industry that the town found its true bent. This expansion suffered a cruel set-back in 1940, when German bombers set fire to the town, destroying two thirds of the buildings. Molde as we know it today has the unmistakable stamp of the 1950's. It is now predominantly a commercial centre. Cars and buses daily bring thousands of eager buyers to the town's many shops and service institutions. Molde's clothing factories, however, still employ many workers, with the

18

furniture and mechanical industry lying a good second. Nor must we forget that Molde, with a number of first-class hotels, is one of Norway's leading tourist resorts. The district college of advanced education teaches economics and administration, transport subjects, computer techniques and mathematics up to university level.

Even in its busiest moments, however, Molde still retains the look of an administrative centre. It has fostered the traditions we associate with the old ruling classes and not least with the town's famous sheriff, the author Alexander L. Kielland. The town has even preserved some of the air of calm and peace which lured Ibsen to these parts. Drifting in a small boat along Fannestrand beach, he composed dramatic scenes, and another famous poet, Bjørnstjerne Bjørnson, went to school in Molde, and found motifs here for many of his works. It was Bjørnson, too, who in 1907 presented and later unveiled the bust of Kielland which now stands in the Reknes park.

We had already mentioned Molde's most glorious attraction, the view of the Romsdal mountains, which is so universally admired. So are the roses. Both can be enjoyed from the roof garden on top of the Town Hall close to Molde Church, impressive with its spacious interior and decor. An overland trip by motor coach and ferry is arranged to Kristiansund, where the ship is rejoined. This cuts out the crossing of Hustadvika, and involves a drive of 70 km, along Fannestranden past Moldegård and other imposing residences, and across Batnfjordeidet, where there are fine views of the mountains in Eikesdalen. A 20-minute ferry crossing takes you to Frei, and the drive concludes with a brisk run over lofty bridges to Kristiansund.

Meantime the coastal express steams north across Julsundet in the direction of Hustadvika. Before reaching the sea we pass between Bjørnsund on the left and picturesque *Bud* on the right. **Bud** Bud is one of Romsdal's well-known fishing villages. It was to Bud in 1533 that Norway's last archbishop Olav Engelbrektsson summoned the Norwegian Council of State as well as representatives of the burgesses and peasants, to elect a king, in a last attempt to assert national independence in the face of Danish dominance.

The passage across Hustadvika calls for careful navigation. The belt of reefs and islands is 2 miles wide, and frequently the channel runs within a stone's throw of the breakers. Even on summer days the buoys emit their weird and hollow warning note, reminding us of the dangers that must lurk on stormy winter nights. A little further on we get a good look at *Hustad,* mentioned in the saga as **Hustad** Hustadir, the royal manor where King Øystein died in 1123. Close at hand lies Hustadfeltet, a large area of land, once waste and untilled, but now turned into smiling cornfields with the aid of modern machines.

19

From the top of Aksla in Ålesund there are views of the islands, the open sea beyond and the fjords as far as the Sunnmøre Alps, as well as a bird's eye wiew of the city.

Built on three islands — Kirkelandet, Innlandet og Nordlandet—separated by narrow sounds and linked together by a series of **Kristiansund** bridges, *Kristiansund* (pop. some 18,000) is a fascinating town fronting the sea.

In 1691 the Dutchman Jappe Ippes, father of the clip-fish, settled in Lille-Fosen, and already the next year the first cargo of the new ware was sent abroad, to be followed by countless others. The town's future was assured, and in a happy moment Jappe named one of his boats "The Golden Clip-Fish". In 1742 Lille-Fosen acquired the rights and charter of a town, and took the name of

Built on a number of islands separated by narrow sounds and linked by a series of bridges, Kristiansund rises on terraces encircling a busy harbour.

Kristiansund. Merchants from Scotland and England settled in the new town, and more and more ships set sail for the Mediterranean with "el bacalao" in their holds, an important item in the fare of Catholic countries on fast days. The ballast, Spanish soil and gravel, was dumped in the harbour at Gomaland, where the old cemetery now lies. During the next 200 years Kristiansund developed into a charming little town, with picturesque wooden houses standing in narrow twisting little alleys. In 1940 Kristiansund was bombed, and 724 houses were destroyed by fire. Most of the old buildings disappeared, but the new ones that have arisen to

21

take their plave have preserved the town's character, and are built in terraces rising up from the harbour. Although there are bridges linking the islands together, local launches still buzz around the harbour in the role of "streetcars".

Kristiansund still exports considerable quantities of clip-fish. The most important local industry is fish-processing. Quite a number of Norway's trawlers, too, are built here, and many have Kristiansund as their home port. Attempts, however, have been made to depend less on the fishing industry, and there has been success in producing textile and clothing, as well as soap and cosmetics. More recently Kristiansund has been drawn into the offshore oil industry with the setting-up of Vestbasen in 1980, a service base for central Norway intended to co-operate with drilling operations on the Halten Bank off the Trøndelag coast. In 1981 promising gas strikes were made in this area. In an entirely different sphere comes Kristiansund's reputation as the scene of an annual opera, produced by enthusiastic local amateurs.

Wharves and the harbour are not the only local attraction. Note the bold lines of the Sørsund Bridge under which we shall be sailing. It is over a quarter of a mile long and just under 120 ft. high. The hatshaped rock, Bremneshatten 500 ft. high, seen through the arch, is pierced with a number of caves, of which the 80-yard Bremnes Cave is the longest. Many tourists consider that the major local attraction is the new church, a fine example of bold Scandinavian architecture; others award the palm to the town hall; others again prefer the Lossiusgaard, on Innlandet, one of three old patrician residences to have survived the bombing of 1940.

The stretch from Kristiansund to Trondheim is described under day 11.

Trondheim to Leka

Trondheim is described under the 11th day of the trip. Northbound an excursion by motor coach is arranged to the Ringve Musical Museum outside Trondheim.

Just outside Trondheim we pass *Munkholmen*. Here in the Middle **Munk-** Ages stood the Nidarholm Abbey, which was abandoned after the **holmen** first fire in 1531, and the last traces of which disappeared when Munkholmen became a fortress in the seventeenth century. When the Swedes occupied Trondheim in 1658 and 1718 the 26 cannon on the island proved singularly ineffective, as the mainland was out of range! At Munkholmen, too, Kristian V's powerful minister, Griffenfeldt, was imprisoned for 18 years (1680–98) after incurring the royal displeasure.

A little further on, to the left, we notice Thamshavn with its ferro-alloy factory, also the export harbour for pyrites from the Løkken Works. The fjord narrows, and we sail past Stadsbygd to the right, and on the same side catch sight of the manor of Reinskloster at Rissa, known to us from the novels of Johan Bojer as Lindegård. Reinskloster was built by Duke Skule, and Sigrid Undset has described the life of the nuns in this abbey in her novel "Kristin Lavransdatter". Lady Inger of Austråt was its patroness round about the year 1500, and at the moment we are heading straight for *Austråt Castle* itself, where this powerful lady, with her **Austråt** many landowning interests, resided. It was from Austråt that she carried on her intrigues with the archbishop and the nobles of the country, in the accepted Renaissance style. The present castle, from the 17th century, is owned by the State. The forest behind Austråt is protected. Here grows the world's northernmost oak, 500–600 years old, probably planted by a Danish nobleman. In this forest there is a fortress from World War II with guns from the "Gneisenau".

The flat country to the west of Austråt is known as *Ørlandet*. The **Ørlandet** soil, at one time below sea-level, provides rich farming land, and the district is densely populated. On the tip of Ørlandet the Norwegian Air Force has built its main air base for the county of Trøndelag. Inside the boundary fences some thousand acres of arable land have been leased to local farmers. A broad belt of soil, one kilometre wide, that was exposed at low tide, has also been reclaimed with the aid of dams and a canal with an ingenious system of pipeline. As a result the entire area of close on 2000 acres that was lost when the airport was built has now been recouped.

On the island of Storfosna stands Storfosen Manor, a royal

manor farm in the Middle Ages and, after Austrât, the biggest farm in the whole of Trøndelag.

Stokksund Later on that day the coastal steamer zig-zags up the narrow twisting *Stokksund Sound*. The first time Kaiser Wilhelm II sailed up this sound on board the "Höhenzollern" the story goes that he lost his head and tried to take the wheel from the pilot. But pilot Nordhus, "The Imperial Pilot", as he was afterwards called, answered imperturbably, "Being a Kaiser won't help you; I'm the pilot here." Be that as it may, the Norwegian pilots certainly do a good job, and Nordhus was awarded a gold watch, bearing the imperial monogram, as a reward for his work.

A special feature of Stokksund is provided by the numerous caves, of which the best known is the Harbak Cave, often used in the past as a place of refuge for fugitives from the law. There are more caves on the island of Stokøya, where the finest bathing beach in Sør-Trøndelag, Hosensanden, is situated. But pride of place along this stretch of coast goes undoubtedly to the Halvik Cave at Osen, a little further north. Some 300 yards from its mouth it broadens into a large lofty hall.

Folda Our ship now crosses *Folda*, the third of the 6 short stretches of open sea in our 1,250 mile journey. Some 50 nautical miles off the coast lies the Halten Bank, where experimental drilling for oil and gas is now going on. Later, in the lee of Gjæslingan, we approach Vikna, a cluster of large and small islands scattered in the ocean west of channel. Between Vikna and the mainland the Nærøysund Sound opens up. Here we sail beneath the 700-metre-long Nærøysund suspension bridge, with a central span of 325 m., the fifth biggest in Norway, with a clearance height of 41 m. Together with the almost 600-m-long bridge across Marøysund, it links the Vikna archipelago with its close on 6,000 islands and skerries to the mainland. In the 1940s 50 of these islands were inhabited. Today the 4000 inhabitants are living on 7 of them, half of them residing in the "capital" at *Rørvik*, where we call in the middle of the sound.

Rørvik Rørvik is the business and communications centre for the Vikna archipelago, with fishing, net mending, a factory for processing seaweed and various service and trading enterprises as the basis for the local economy. Practically all shipping and fishing vessels along this coast pass through the Nærøysund, and not surprisingly attempts have been made to cater to the needs of this traffic. Rørvik is also one of the stations manned by the Norwegian salvage company, and the tall masts are those of the coastal radio station.

The narrow passage at Rørvik is the gateway to the Nordland channel, which according to ancient myth and popular superstition was once the battle ground of giants and trolls and their womenfolk. One of the many

"Nordre," Trondheim's busy thoroughfare and promenade, is generally thronged with busy crowds. This is the street where people go to see and be seen, and, of course, to shop.

myths dealing with these super-natural beings runs as follows: There was once a troll-king, reigning in Lofoten, whose name was Vågekallen. On the mainland lived the king of Sulitjelma. Vågekallen had a dare-devil and high-spirited son called Hestmannen (The Horseman), and the king of Sulitjelma had seven wild and giddy daughters. One day these daughters went to visit the old woman of Landego with the fair Lekamøya, and one evening, when they were bathing naked in the sea, Hestmannen caught sight of them. The beauty of Lekamøy inflamed him, and at midnight he rode off on his horse to seize her and bear her away. Just in time the girls saw him coming, and they fled southward down the channel. The king of

25

Sømnafjell near Brønnøysund was roused by the noise, and just as the baffled and infuriated Hestmannen drew his bow to send an arrow after the fleeing maidens, the king threw his hat in the way. At that moment the sun came up, and all the trolls were petrified, including the hat which was pierced by the arrow, and has ever since been called the Torghatt.

Fair Lekamøy is the first one of the petrified figures of myth to greet us. This mountain, which is an old landmark, lies on the **Leka** southern tip of the island of *Leka*, not far from the Solsem cave with its Stone Age rock drawings. Further north, near the church, Norway's second large burial mound rises 8–10 m. above the ground. This is a Viking ship grave, and archaeologists believe that one of the powerful Namdøl earls lies buried here.

Leka has one special claim to fame. It was here that a four-year-old child was seized by an eagle, in the summer of 1932, and carried off to a nearby mountain top over a thousand feet above the valley. Svanhild, as the girl was called, is still alive and recalls her adventure. Recently ornithologists have cast doubts on the authenticity of the story, and heated arguments were carried on in the media. So much so that in 1979 a committee was set up at Leka to combat the unbelievers.

In the summer's evening we glide up the Leka Fjord. Just before crossing the county boundary into Nordland we catch a glimpse of the challenging Mount Heilhorn on our right. If the weather is clear we should now have Torghatten ahead, and far ahead the Seven Sisters. The very landscape is redolent with the spirit of old myths and fairy tales. Soon we pass the mouth of the Bindalfjord. The people of the Bindalfjord are not only famed for their skill in building small boats, but also produce considerable quantities of timber. In addition they catch great numbers of salmon. Fifty years ago there was a veritable gold rush in the Bindal Mountains. Small quantities of the precious metal were discovered, but no workable seam was ever localised. The high price of gold on the world market has now resulted in experimental drilling in the old mines.

The stretch from Leka to Hestmannøy (Horseman Island) is described under day 10.

FOURTH DAY:

Hestmannøy to Raftsund

Cruising up the coast of Nordland one gets the impression that fishing is the chief source of livelihood in the north. This, however, is not the case. Statistics show that about one quarter of the working population is employed in each of the following: industry and construction work; trade and transport; administration and services. Only one in 7 works on the land and one in fourteen onboard fishing vessels. But it should again be emphasised that thousands of jobs on land are created and maintained by the needs of the fishing fleet. Previously fishing and farming often went hand in hand: a farmer would earn a little extra on the winter fisheries, while many fishermen cultivated a patch of ground. Those days are all but gone. Capital investments in both of these activities are now so big that fishing and farming must be considered full-time occupations. Industry has only recently set its seal on North Norway. Before the last war mining was carried on in Salten and Rana on a small scale, and various fish processing factories were spread over the county. After the war great changes have taken place: an iron steel plant has been built at Mo i Rana, an aluminium "town" has sprung up at Mosjøen, while Glomfjord is the site of a large plant set up by Norsk Hydro. Of the approx. 10,000 GWh produced by the country's power stations over one half is consumed by power-demanding industry.

The population of Nordland is just under 250,000.

Our journey continues. Early in the morning we pass the Arctic Circle at 66 degrees 33 minutes North or 27 degrees 27 minutes from the North Pole and we are now in the Land of the Midnight Sun. The Arctic Circle passes through the island of *Hestmannøy* **Hestmannøy** (Horseman Island), an old acquaintance from the myth related above. Should you ever feel the urge to scale the 568 m Hestmann, you ought to know that the going is fairly easy as far as the "neck", and that this is followed by a scary section, a sheer cliff of some hundreds of metres, where a rope is highly recommended. The top itself is as flat as a pancake, and the view across a sea sprinkled with myriad islands and skerries is the due reward of the bold climber. As we turn to the right we get Selsøyvik to the north, one of the old harbours that lay dotted along the ancient channel. The costal steamer was unable to call there, and the modern age has passed it by.

We shall be passing many similar spots: Støtt, Nord-Arnøy, Grøtøy, Storvågen, Kløven, etc. These places were originally obliged to provide accommodation and shelter for travellers, and for that reason they were situated approx. a day's journey apart. Most of them fell into disuse not only as a result of the coming of the coastal steamer to serve North Norway at the end of the last century, but also with the expansion of the road net-work. Today many of them breathe an air of remote charm, and seem to dream of

27

One of the narrowest passages negotiated by the coastal express is Stokksund. Near the exit can be seen the 130-metre-deep Harbakhulen cave situated on the mainland.

Nærøysund is the actual gateway to the fairytale world of the Nordland channel. Here the coastal express calls at Rørvik, the administrative hub of an archipelago of 6,000 islands and skerries.

the days when they played an important part in the economic life of this part of Norway. The channel was the royal route to the north, and the only one. Even by modern standards the traffic which passed this way was considerable. One fifth of the entire population of the counties of Troms and Nordland came to Lofoten for the fishing season, and in addition every spring and autumn the Nordland boats took their fish to the great markets in Bergen.

Rødøyløven   To the left another peculiar mountain island rises out of the sea—*Rødøyløven*—a 440-metre-high sphinx of serpentine. Although it is not mentioned in our myth, it is regarded as one of the major attractions of the Nordland channel.

Svartisen   From now on we can see the *Svartisen Glacier* rising inland. This glacier, with an area of 200 square miles, is Norway's second largest ice field. The highest point on the glacier is Snøtind, 5,300 ft. above sea level. Cruising liners generally make a detour up the Holand Fjord to give passengers a sight of the Engabre, an arm of the mighty Svartisen glacier. In 1974 the foot of the glacier terminated 100 m above sea-level, but since then Svartisen has moved closer to the sea, and by now there is only a difference of 10–12 m in altitude between the fjord and the glacier. We sail past *Grønøy*, which really means Green Island, a low and luxuriant slate island, and Meløy, which in the 16th century belonged to the Danish Benkestok family, and formed the nucleus of their tremendous estates. The male line became extinct in the 17th century, but there is a Benkestok strain in most of the better-known families of Nordland. Thus descendants

Ørnes   of the Benkestoks once owned *Ørnes*—the old port from 1794 for which we are now making—right up to the present. Though the main building of the old trading post burnt down during the last war, the cluster of houses retains its original appearance from 1805. From Ørnes there is a road to Glomfjord, where Norsk Hydro produces ammonia, fertilizers, nitric acid and heavy water. Fiskklipp at Ørnes not surprisingly produce klip-fish.

Many harsh words have been said about the merchants who owned the old trading centres: they have been accused of keeping the fishermen in a state of economic subservience, but the judgment of history is less harsh, and probably more just. At a time when little money was in circulation and no proper system of credit had been established, the merchants were an indispensible part of the social structure. They were the only people who could advance equipment and goods to the fishermen, with future catches as security. Many fishermen in those days, of course, were almost continually in debt to the local merchant, but most of these local big-wigs evinced a benevolent and patriarchal spirit whenever there was a bad fishing season. Nor should we forget that these merchants, together with the professional classes and the land-owners, were the bearers of culture who left many traces behind, not least in the beautiful buildings they erected.

30

A little further north we sail past Størt, another of the forgotten ports along the channel, and round the dreaded Kunna promontory, once the boundary between Helgeland and Salten, which the open Nordland boats found so difficult to negotiate. Many ships have gone down off Kunna. The remains of a Dutch boat which foundered with all hands in the 1920s can still be seen. Later, on the mainland to the right, we catch sight of Gildeskål Church, built about 1130, with a south wing added in 1711. Looking towards Fugløya we shall observe a strange natural phenomenon, sand whirled up by the wind and streaming down the mountainside like a waterfall. Below the characteristic Sandhorn (3,300 ft.) at Våg on *Sandhornøy* lies Blixgård Manor, and as we steam past we can see the **Sandhornøy** memorial raised to the poet Elias Blix. His work as Professor of Hebrew, Bible translator and Minister of Ecclesiastical Affairs has long been forgotten, but he will always be remembered as the author of the national song «Å eg veit meg eit land» (O, I know of a land). Before we cross the Salt Fjord we catch a glimpse of Nordarnøy to the left, yet another of the once frequented ports of call.

On the mainland south of the Saltfjord we catch sight of the attractive shapes of the Børvasstind Peaks (3,900 ft.). At their foot the Saltstraum runs through a sound which is two miles long and 150 yards wide, separating the Salt Fjord from the Skjerstad Fjord. When the tide flows the water is pressed with tremendous force through the sound, producing the celebrated natural phenomenon which is a well-known tourist attraction. The Moskenesstraum in the Lofotens has won literary fame as the notorious "maelstrom" (e.g.in the works of Edgar Allan Poe, Jules Verne, etc.) but the Saltstraum is more impressive.

Bodø, capital town of the county of Nordland, is pleasantly **Bodø** situated on the western corner of the Bodin peninsula, against a magnificent background of mountains. Trading and fishing establishments inaugurated by the merchants of Trondheim around the year 1800 provided the nucleus for the present town, and an Act of the Storting of 1816 gave Bodø the rights and privileges of a town.

Some years later a remarkable incident, known as the Bodø affair, caused considerable upheavals in the little community. An English firm of merchants who had established themselves in Bodø were accused of illegal trade and unscrupulous business methods, and the customs confiscated their wares. The English merchants, however, overpowered the customs officials, and made off with the goods. Later on the English merchants sued the Swedish-Norwegian Foreign Minister for damages in Stockholm, and it was agreed that the Norwegians should pay compensation to the tune of £ 18,000. This decision aroused a great deal of hostility against the English, but even more bitterness against the Swedes, who according to the

The Horseman is a popular figure in local myth and legends. At this point we cross the arctic circle and enter the realm of the Midnight Sun.

Svartisen, Norway's second largest glacier, has grown in recent years, and now only vertical 10–12 metres separates it from the sea in the Holand Fjord.

Norwegians had failed to protect Norwegian interests. The Bodø affair had considerable repercussions, as it became an issue in Norway's demands for a separate Foreign Service. To complete this story we should mention that the English firm maintained that its business in Bodø was legal, and that the accusations levelled against them had been inspired by rival traders from Bergen and Trondheim.

The new township expanded slowly: 20 years after its inception there were only 200 inhabitants, but in the 1860's and 70's its growth was hastened by the tremendous herring fisheries which were opened up, and proved an important factor in the economic liberation of this part of Norway. Mining at Sulitjelma and the inception of the coastal steamer were an added spur. Trade flourished, new factories connected with the fishing industry sprang up, and shipping rose in importance.

During the German bombardment of Bodø in May, 1940, 420 of the town's 760 houses were destroyed and 3,700 people were rendered homeless. Bodø was spaciously and attractively rebuilt after the war. Its assets included a fine harbour and good steamship connections. In 1937 the North Norway Highway had been extended from the south to reach Bodø. After the war rail and air links with the rest of the country were added. Trade, tourism, industry and the service trades flourished, and the town has increased its population and its area. In fact in the course of 25 years the population has trebled and now stands at about 32,500. Bodø is a typical business and administrative centre, with almost twice as many persons engaged in these sectors as in industry and construction. It houses the county administration, the North Norway Defence HQ with various staffs and units, and the Sør-Hålogaland episcopal see. The regional college of advanced education and a pedagogical high school are prominent in the educational sector.

Bodø Cathedral, a triple-nave basilica with a "detached" tower, was consecrated in 1956. This outstanding example of modern church architecture is well worth a visit. Outside the Nordland Museum one can see a fine specimen of a "fembøring" fishing boat. Inside is an attractively presented collection featuring fishing.

From the restaurant at Rørvikfjell there is a wonderful view in the direction of Værøy, Lofoten, and Landego to the north-west, Kjerringøy to the north-east, Fleinvær, Sandhornet, Kunna, and Fugløy to the south-west, and Børvasstindan to the south-east. Mount Rørvikfjell is only 2 miles from Bodø and reached in a few minutes by taxi. The Midnight Sun is visible here from June 3 to July 8.

We have already heard the name of *Landego,* just outside Bodø, from our myth. This name is really a taboo used by seamen to

ensure a good passage in from *Vestfjord,* the fourth of the open Vestfjorden
stretches of sea along our route. If you have a good look you may
spot the "Landego Man" climbing up the mountain from the sea on
the extreme north side of the island. From Skomvær lighthouse to
the south-west, and as far as Tjeldsund to the north-east, the Vest
Fjord measures 120 miles. In bad weather this bay is nasty, but in
fine weather the three-hour journey across the open sea is one of the
delights of the trip. Astern we can see the mountains running inland
as far as Sulitjelma. Far out to the west lies Røst, which contains as
many islands and grassy holms as there are days in the year. At
Røst some of the largest colonies of sea birds in the world have their
homes. The most recent counts show close on one million pairs of
puffins, also called sea-parrots. In addition there are kittiwake,
gannet and stormy petrels (not recorded elsewhere in Norway) and
a small number of fulmar. Especially puffins failed to nest in the
years 1974 to 1982, almost certainly because their source of food –
small herring – was scarce. In 1983 the herring was again available,
and the young birds survived. Incidentally, the temperature at Røst
never falls below zero as a mean average in winter. On the islands
there are 78 summer days, from June 27 to September 12, with
mean temperature over 10° Centigrade. To the landward side of
Røst, Værøy rises from the sea. Mostad on Værøy has some 80,000
pairs of puffin. Between Mosken and Lofotodden runs the
Moskenesstream, which inspired such thriller writers as Poe and
Jules Verne.

Some five miles north of Landego we have — due east on the
mainland — the old trading post of Kjerringøy, known as Sirilund
in Knut Hamsun's novels. It is now a museum. It was here that the
TV series *Rosa and Benoni,* based on Hamsun's novels, was filmed.
For many fishermen in days gone by bound for the Lofotens
Kjerringøy was the last port-of-call. At times hundreds of boats
would be lying in the sound, waiting for a fair wind.

The jagged peaks of the *Lofoten Wall* come nearer and nearer. **Lofoten Wall**
This great bastion stretches for 60 miles from Lofotodden on the
extreme tip of Moskenesøy all the way to Raftsund Sound. The
mountains consist of granites and volcanic rock. During the last Ice
Age the Lofotens were subject to severe glacial action, and when the
ice disappeared the landscape was revealed as one of exceptionally
wild Alpine grandeur.

Stamsund, situated on the island of Vestvågøy, is the creation of **Stamsund**
one man, Julius M. Johansen, who went to work with a vengeance
at the beginning of the century, blasting a site for the fishing village
in the barren mountain side. Up-to-date quays, modern fishing
equipment, a codliver-oil refinery, shops, fishermen's shelters, and
even a church, were built at the orders of this self-made man, who

Above the old trading centre at Ørnes the Spilder Horse cavorts.

became Norway's greatest producer of dried fish and guano. Today the fourth generation of this enterprising family are connected with the firm. Stamsund presently boasts two of the largest fish-producing enterprises in the Lofotens, as a well as company operating nine trawlers.

As we sail along the Lofoten Wall we might mention that every summer tourists from many lands make their way here to enjoy a holiday in a so-called *rorbu*, a fisherman's shanty with the necessary equipment, etc., for a do-it-yourself vacation. Among the many who have enjoyed this kind of holiday are the former Norwegian Prime Minister and the former German Chancellor Helmut Schmidt.

Landego near Bodø has a well-known profile. The name originates in an ancient tabu among seafaring men and fishermen anxious to flatter the gods of old by calling the seaward approach "good".

Henningsvær, where free trade reigned supreme during the **Henningsvær** fisheries before 1962 and anybody could put up a shop, clings tenaciously to a number of small islands between Stamsund and Svolvær. This is one of the most typical fishing villages in the Lofoten islands, where more than 6,000 fishermen used to be based during the Lofoten fisheries in former days. The quaintly-shaped mountain behind Henningsvær on Austvågøy is the *Vågekallen* **Vågekallen** (3,100 ft.). Vågekallen is not only an excellent landmark, but offers first-rate climbing. This peak was first scaled in 1889. Locally it is held in veneration, and the young fisher lad who joins the Lofoten fisheries for the first time is obliged to take his hat off to Vågekallen. On the mountain can be seen a stone figur which is remarkably like a fisherman with a spar under his arm.

Kabelvåg Between Vågekallen and Svolvær lies *Kabelvåg*, the oldest fishing village in the Lofotens. In 1120 King Øystein decreed that "rorbuer" should be built at Kabelvåg, and later King Håkon Håkonssons ordered the men of Nordland to use it as a trading centre. In the 19th century Kabelvåg was the biggest fishing village in the Lofotens. Vågan Church built in 1898, and designed to seat 1200 worshippers, was alway filled to capacity during the fisheries. This was probably the sixth church in Vågan. The first was erected by King Øystein Magnusson (1088–1123), according to the Sagas. The present church in Vågan is the largest timber-built church north of Trondheim.

Svolvær The neighbouring village of *Svolvær* has also existed ever since the Middle Ages, and with its deep and ramified harbour it has superseded Kabelvåg as the leading fishing village in the Lofotens. Today Svolvær has more than 4,000 inhabitants, but at the height of the fishing season the population used to increase many-fold. On occasions as many as 10,000 fishermen have set out from Svolvær for the banks.

The Lofoten fisheries take place on the shallow coastal banks just off the islands from January to the end of April, with March usually as the busiest month. Only 30 years ago 20,000 to 30,000 fishermen and four to five thousand boats took part in the fisheries. To-day some 4000–5000 fishermen and some 1000 boats are engaged, and in recent years the catch has amounted to 40–50 million kilos. The "old-fashioned" handlines, nets and longlines account for the greatest total catch, but the most efficient type for equipment that has been used is the purse net, which has been known to make a haul of 50–60,000 kilos at one cast. Previously, too, annual catches might vary from 20 to 150 million kilos. In those days the economy of Nordland revolved around the Lofoten fisheries, and according to an old saying a poor season had repercussions all the way down to Karl Johan, Oslo's main street.

Lofoten has an abiding charm for the artist, the light and the local colour being the main attractions. The district's own painter is the Svolvær-born Gunnar Berg. Painters such as Werenskiold, Kittelsen, Revold and Rolfsen have also produced canvasses depicting these fishing villages. But no one has captured the great drama of the Lofotens more strikingly than Kaare Espolin Johnson with his special "scraping technique". His Petter Dass freize on board the coastal express steamer *Harald Jarl*, which also includes motives from the Lofotens, is an outstanding example. Today a small colony of painters live at Svolvær in the recently constructed artists' house at Svinøya, which has accommodation for six Swedish and six Norwegian painters. There is also an art centre with exibition premises and studios. But the appeal to the writer has been just as strong—Johan Bojer has described fishing in the olden days, Carl Schøyen has depicted life in the fishing villages, and on the rocky islands, and Andreas Markusson and Edvard Welle-Strand have dealt with fishing in the age of the powered fishing smack.

Many people will remember the Commando raids on the Lofotens during the last war. The first, on March 4th, 1941, was directed against Svolvær. Henningsvær, Stamsund and Brettesnes. The object of this raid was to destroy the herring oil factories to prevent the Germans from using the oil for glycerine which they needed for munitions. The striking force consisted of 5 destroyers. two transports and 600 commandoes. Many volunteers returned with the raiders to England to join the Norwegian forces, and German reprisals against the civilian population followed. The object of the second raid, in December 1941, at Reine, was to establish a temporary base for light naval units which should attack and seek to interrupt German sea communications to the Murmansk front and hinder the transit of iron ore from Narvik. 21 ships and some 500 troops were engaged in the operation. Landing took place on December 26th, but only two days later the force withdrew after Admiral Hamilton had received reports of Luftwaffe reinforcement in North Norway, especially at Bodø on the other side of the Vest Fjord. The abrupt withdrawal caused great disappointment among the locals and the participating units. Churchill, who had eagerly supported the operation, was "disappointed over the results and critical of the decision to withdraw".

The coastal steamer worms its way out from Svolvær, and gives us a view of Svolværgeita (The Svolvær Goat), an approx. 130-foot "needle" poised 2,000 ft. above the town's cemetery and scaled for the first time in 1910. Between its horns the "goat" measures five feet, and the expert climber gets an extra thrill out of jumping from Storhornet (the big horn) to Lillehornet (the little horn). On our starboard beam we see Skrova, for long the busiest fishing village in the Lofotens, owing to its proximity to the fishing grounds. Today Skrova leads the way in the hunting of minor cetaceans. From May until well into autumn whaling employs 150 hands. This form of whaling was started in the Vest Fjord in the 1920's. In the olden days boats making their way from Grøtøy across the Vest Fjord always set a course for Skrova.

The stretch from Raftsund to Harstad is described under day 9.

On the banks off the Lofotens cod fishing has been carried on since the dawn of history. Fishing usually culminates in March, with thousands of fishermen and their boats gathered in local harbours.

Svolvær with its excellent harbour is the "capital" of the Lofotens. This is a view of the town from Svolværgeita, the Svolvær Goat.

41

Harstad to Lyngen

Harstad   *Harstad* is beautifully situated on the north-east side of Hinnøy, Norway's largest island. This town flourished during the rich herring-fishing years of the last century, thanks to its good harbour. A fruitful hinterland assisted the process, and in 1903 it acquired the privileges of a "ladested" (township). Later it has acquired a number of industries. In fact more than half of the entire engineering industry of North Norway is situated in Harstad. Here is to be found the only floating dock in this part of Norway, numerous shipbuilding and repair yards, cold storage and refrigeration plant, North Norway's biggest dairy and large meat-processing factories. Not surprisingly Harstad has been selected as one of the bases for the North Norway offshore oil industry. Several oil companies have already established themselves in the town. Prospecting for oil and gas is proceeding with the aid of two rigs on the Tromsøflak bank during the summer months, and good strikes have already been made. "Greater" Harstad has 21,500 inhabitants, while the actual town itself has a population of about 5,000. Industry, farming and fishing together with shipping and transport employ the vast majority of the local labour force. Practically every day foreign trawlers call there to re-fuel, re-provision, and carry out minor repairs. Today the presence of supply vessels carrying provisions and equipment to offshore oil rigs adds a novel touch to the busy life of the harbour. The lively fish export and trade that goes on also gives Harstad an air of bustle, while the fact that several military headquarters and an officers training school are assembled in Harstad also makes it into a garrison town.

At the end of June every year the North Norway Festival, with its concerts, plays, and various exhibitions, brings a spate of visitors to town. In July this is rivalled by the traditional sea-fishing competition. The Midnight Sun is an added attraction, visible from May 23 to July 22. Finally: northbound and southbound coastal express steamer meet in Harstad. Make sure you board the right one. People have made a mistake.

Harstad's greatest attraction is *Trondenes Church*, situated just outside the town boundary. The saga relates that King Øystein had a church built at Trondenes during the 12th century. The original church was probably a wooden building. The present church is from 1250, and is remarkable for the fact that it is a fortress church, with walls over 8 feet thick. The stone wall surrounding the church, which in places is sixteen foot tall, and the remains of two watchtowers on the seaward side, tend to confirm this impression.

The 15th century altar screens are also unique, especially the main altar. The font is from the Middle Ages, and on the walls can be seen the remains of old chalk paintings, as well as twelve dedicatory crosses, one for each apostle. The vaults beneath the church contain several coffins, one of which is dated 1691. In the Middle Ages Trondenes was Norway's northernmost stone church, and undoubtedly one of the most important in the country in Roman Catholic times. Already in the Viking Age Trondenes was a local meeting place, and the county "ting" or parliament met there. During the 11th century Sigurd Hund, brother of Tore Hund, lived at Trondenes. Sigurd was married to the daugther of Erling Skjalgsson. Among other well-known Norwegians born at Trondenes might be mentioned Norway's last archbishop, Olav Engelbrektsson, and "the Greenland Apostle", Hans Egede.

Leaving Harstad we steam north across the Vågs Fjord. Before entering the Solberg Fjord we catch sight of *Bjarkøy* on the left. **Bjarkøy**

Tore Hund founded the vast fortunes of the Bjarkøy family by trading with Laplanders and Carelians, and systematic looting. Tore Hund was originally King Olav the Saint's liegeman, but became his bitterest enemy when the king had his nephew Asbjørn Selsbane put to death. The lord of Bjarkøy now became leader of the opposition against St. Olav, the king who set out to convert Norway to Christianity and was also anxious to crush the power of the old aristocracy, of which Tore was one of the leading representatives. According to Snorre, the saga writer, Tore was one of the men who struck the king down at Stiklestad in the year 1030. Erling Vidkunsson was a member of the Bjarkøy clan, and was born on the island. He was Norway's great political leader at the beginning of the 14th century, and acted as Regent during the minority of Magnus Erlingsson. In 1952, during excavations on the island of Bjarkøy, a dwelling site, consisting of 16 large and a number of smaller houses, was discovered.

Bjarkøy was once one of Norway's most important sources of eiderdown, and the eggs of sea birds were also collected here in large numbers. The population took good care of the eider duck, even building homes for the more gregarious birds in old boats, while the more individualistic birds were provided with desirable detached residences in empty crates. In return for this kindness they provided large quantities of valuable eiderdown.

By now we have discovered some of the characteristic features of the county of Troms. The county of Troms is the middle county, sharing some of the topographical characteristics of Nordland and Finnmark, with an economic set-up that reflects some of the features of both these counties. Industry figures less prominently, while farming, as in Nordland, employs about one seventh of the working population and fishing a little under one

The oil age has reached Harstad, which is one of the supply bases for prospecting on the Norwegian continental shelf, and several companies have established themselves here.

tenth. Even so fishing must be regarded as a major pillar of the economy, as it provides a great many jobs in fish processing and sales. As a fisherman and a seaman the man of Troms is of a piece with the man of Sunnmøre, aiming to keep up his fishing all the year round. You find him up and down the Norwegian coast when the large fisheries are on, off the coast of Iceland, on the Greenland banks, and in the Barents Sea, as well as taking his share of the cod that teem on the Svendsgrunn and Malangsgrunn banks. He also catches seal in the Greenland pack-ice. However, few men of Troms are still working in such colourful and perilous vocations. In common with most of the labour force of the western world they are to be found in construction building and industry, retail trade, transport and public and private

Through the morning mist magic mountains appear, perfect pyramid shapes like Rolla east of Harstad.

administration and services. Three areas that have recorded a marked growth in recent years are education, health and defence. The first two are due to the establishment of the University of Tromsø, while the increase in defence commitments is due to the need to protect NATO's northern flank, which is concentrated on this region of mountains and fjords.

Senja, Norway's second largest island, presents a cross-section of the county, with trim farms on the landward side, bleak fishing villages on the seaward side, and with some of the best fishing banks in Norway just off the coast. The fairway inbetween Senja and the mainland is blithe, lush, and green, with pleasant farmland framed

45

Finnsnes in deciduous woods. As we run up Gisund Sound we see *Finnsnes* on a small promontory sticking out into the channel. The old trading centre of Kløven on the other side of the sound was abandoned when Finnsnes was linked by road to the inland districts and also became a coastal steamer port. Today Finnsnes is a sizable urban community, with a factory turning out fishing tackle and accessories as one of its major enterprises, the other being the Fesil-Nord smelting works with an annual capacity of some 50,000 tons of ferro-silicium. The bridge between Finnsnes and Senja is the longest pillar bridge in Europe, 1150 metres long.

At the narrowest part of the Gisund Sound lies the old trading post, Gibostad, with it agricultural college on the left, and Lenvik church on the right. Some experts believe that the celebrated voyager Ottar lived at Gibostad, while others maintain that he dwelt at Tussøy, to the west of Kvaløy, where several interesting archaeological finds have been made.

Round about the year 800 Ottar carried out a combined voyage of discovery and trade, past North Cape and eastwards to Kola in the White Sea. This voyage has come down to us because Ottar subsequently served King Alfred of England, and the king considered his account so remarkable that he incorporated Ottar's voyage in his edition of Orosius' History of the World, which is now preserved in the British Museum in Alfred's own handwriting. Ottar maintained that he lived further north than any other Norseman, and he told King Alfred that he was one of the leading men of Hålogaland. He owned 20 cows, 20 sheep, 20 pigs and 600 head of reindeer, according to his own words.

In the days of Ottar, and for centuries afterwards, Malangen was Norway's northernmost boundary and the church at Lenvik the most northerly in the whole country, right up to the time when King Håkon Håkonsson ordered a church to be built on Troms **Rystraumen** island. The coastal express after crossing Malangen enters *Rystraumen*, the swiftest of all the tidal currents on our voyage, which often reaches a speed of 6 knots. Much frequented by saithe, it is a favourite spot for anglers using a spinner. The scenery is now wilder. To the east of Balsfjord the impressive Tverbotnfjell (4,300 ft.) rears up, while to the south of the fjord we have Svartnestind (4,200 ft.) and to the west Slettind (3,700 ft.)

On the island of Tromsøy, in the middle of the channel, lies the **Tromsø** town of *Tromsø*. Tromsø's population figures – 46,000 – need to be explained. The point is that only one third of the inhabitants are to be found in the old urban centre on the island of Tromsøya; another third live on the outskirts, both on the island and the mainland, while the remainder are spread over outlying areas, in the largest urban community in Norway, covering some 960 square miles, and comprising within its confines fishing villages, farming land and reindeer pasture.

It was in about 1250 that King Håkon Håkonsson, as already mentioned, commissioned the building of a church at Tromsø, but it was not until the merchants of North Norway were free to trade on equal terms with the towns of the south that Tromsø prospered. By the time it had become a township in 1794 the privileged position of Bergen and Trondheim had been undermined by the barter trade with Russia and the setting up of inns, which from 1770 on had resulted in a number of trading centres being established in Troms. The town owed its prosperity to the large amount of traffic that passed through the Tromsøy Sound. In 1820 it equipped the first Arctic sealing ships, and the fish export trade grew apace hand in hand with the development of local shipping.

Tromsø today is very much an educational centre, with some 13,000 pupils in 17 different kinds of school, as well as a trading, shipping and service centre. Local industry is based mainly on fisheries, canning, cold storage and refrigerator plant and processing factories, foodstuffs and shipbuilding. Exports are dominated by fish products and furs. And naturally a large number of people are employed in administration, as this is the seat of the various county offices, the county governor, an episcopal see, a regional broadcasting station and a naval district command.

And the climate? Winter lasts a long time in the "Capital of the Arctic", from about November 16 to April 12, when the mean average temperature is below zero. The snow lasts still longer — as much as 180 days. But at the end of May the cowslip rears its head and the sallow is in bloom. Summer heralds its arrival in mid-June with mean average temperatures over 10° C., and lasts till the end of August. Seventy-six days may not seem much, but many of these days are really "doubles", with sunshine right round the clock. The Midnight Sun is visible from May 21 to July 23.

In 1812 an action was fought in the Tromsøy Sound between long-boats belonging to an English frigate and two small Norwegian naval cutters. The next engagement that took place near Tromsø occurred on 12th November, 1944, when the German battleship Tirpitz was attacked and sunk by British planes at Kvaløy after the ship had been under the observation of Norwegian agents. During the war Tromsø acted for a short while as the capital of Free Norway. It was on June 7th, 1940, that the King and the Government were forced to leave the town and the country.

Tromsø has long been a port of departure for expeditions to the Arctic. Elling Carlsen of Tromsø was the first skipper to circumnavigate Svalbard, and it was here that the American Wellman set off with his strange dirigible on board, and that Andrée and his

The Rystraum tiderace south of Tromsø sometimes runs at six knots. This is the fiercest current the coastal express has to cope with on its long voyage.

Tromsø, situated on the island of Tromsøya, is linked to the mainland by a bridge. In 1968 the world's northernmost university was established here.

comrades started their ill-fated voyage. Roald Amundsen looked in on his trips on board the "Gjøa" and "Maud", and it was from Tromsø that he set out on his last flight with the French plane "Latham" on 18th June 1928, when he went to the assistance of the Italian Umberto Nobile. Roald Amundsen's statue stands in a small park near the quay. These links with the frozen wastes of the far north are emphasized by the existence of such institutions as the Northern Lights Observatory, and Tromsø Museum with its fine collections from North Norway and the Arctic. These institutions are now part of the University of Tromsø — the world's northernmost, of course, with some 1,200 students who are taught medicine, science, philology, sociology and fisheries. The Museum, which also has its own marine biological station with aquariums, is visited on one of the two excursions arranged for passengers on board the costal express. The other excursion includes a trip across the one-kilometre-long Tromsø Bridge, pride of the town, to the cable car running up to Storsteinen, 1400 ft. above the sea, with superb views of the surroundings, weather permitting. Perhaps we should mention that Tromsø possesses the world's northernmost brewery, and that this unique firm runs Norway's only "pub" in the real English sense of the world.

The Tromsøy Sound, which is spanned by the big bridge, is one of the coastal "main roads", much frequented by Arctic trappers, trawlers, coastal steamers, freighters and fishing vessels. Big cruising ships have to pass through the Sandnes Sound and under the 1220-metre-long Sandnessund Bridge which runs across to Kvaløya.

Tromsø has produced a number of important writers: it was here that Jonas Lie spent his childhood and the outstanding Norwegian authoress of the post-war years, Cora Sandel (Sara Fabricius), was also a native of Tromsø. Matti Aikio, who described the life of the Lapps, went to Tromsø Seminary and Bernt Lie and Lars Hansen were natives of this town.

Sailing northward up the Tromsø Channel in the late afternoon we can admire the town's Fløyfjell and Tromsdalstind (4,100 ft.) on the mainland. We are also struck by the bold lines of Tromsdalen Church, often referred to as the "Cathedral of the Arctic". In the lee of Kvaløy, Ringvassøy, Reinøy and Karlsøy, we continue our journey through Troms county. Karlsøy was the home of the politically-minded parson, Alfred Eriksen, who was one of the first socialist members of parliament, elected in 1903 on the crest of a radical wave which swept North Norway after several successive years of poor fishing. Karlsøy is also easily distinguishable owing to the very distinct beachlines surviving from the period when the land lay from 50 to 100 feet lower. And now to the east we catch sight of

the *Lyngen* Mountains in all their glory. They are composed of the **Lyngen**
same dark gabbro stone which we find in the Jotunheim range.
With its many peaks it is considered by climbers to be one of
Europe's most exciting ranges, where every expedition can be
certain of still finding virgin ground. Later in the evening the
steamer draws level with Lyngstuva. To the south we can look into
the wild and forbidding Lyngen Fjord. Looking out to sea we can
observe Fugløy rising out of the ocean, where hundreds of
thousands of sea birds nest in colonies. Not infrequently houses out
there blew down, like so many card-houses unless the owners took
the precaution of anchoring them with struts and cables. The island
is now uninhabited.

The stretch Skjervøy to Hammerfest is described under day 8.

SIXTH DAY:

North Cape

In 1681 the citizens of Bergen leased Finnmark at the rate of 200 dollars a
year, payable to the Royal Treasury. At the same time Finnmark became a
place of exile: vagrants and vagabonds and people condemned to
imprisonment could be sent there to work in the fisheries. This part of
Norway was in truth regarded as the Ultima Thule, the extreme north.
Towards the end of the 18th century new economic ideas made their
influence felt. Trade in Finnmark was liberated, the towns of Hammerfest
and Vardø were ordered to be built, and a new era began for this neglected
and backward part of Norway.

Finnmark is a barren county, as the passenger on the deck of the express
steamer will see at a glance; nevertheless it is by no means as unfruitful as
the coastal districts would lead one to believe. This northernmost county of
Norway is a land of contrasts, for there is also a Finnmark of trim farms and
meadows set in wooded valleys·through which the Pasvik, Tana and
Karasjok rivers flow. Between the coast and the Tana valley the whole
country is an unbroken mountain plateau rising to some 300–400 metres,
dotted with well stocked lakes and clad in sparse vegetation, barely
sufficient to provide winter pasture for the county's close on 100,000
domesticated reindeer. Everything in Finnmark is on the grand scale: vast
tracts of moorland, deep fjords, mighty rivers. Biggest of all is the Arctic
Ocean washing its shores, but without its rich fishing banks life would have
been an almost impossible struggle up here in the far north.

Fishing was for long the dominant feature of the local economy, but today
only about one out of ten persons employed can be found actually working
on board a fishing vessel. Even so, the spin-offs from fishing provide a great
many jobs, so that it would be true to say that the bulk of local industry is

The Lyngen peaks are a belt of alpine mountains seventy km long and two km wide. With their glaciers and coombs they comprise a range unmatched in the whole of North Norway.

associated in some way or other with fishing. Industry together with mining, building and construction work employs about one-third of the labour force. Surprisingly enough, in these latitudes, where grain does not ripen, farming has secured a foothold. Thanks to imports of artificial cattle feed, considerable quantities of meat and milk are produced, and this, hand in hand with a certain amount of forestry, employs almost as many hands as the number of persons who make a living on the sea. The remainder of the labour is employed in trade and transport, public administration, private and public services, and the armed forces. All these, which in the widest sense of the term could be termed services trades, account for one half of the work places in the county.

The mountain Lapps trek to the coast with their reindeer every spring, returning to the Finnmark plateau in autumn.

The Lapps have for centuries been a characteristic feature of the local population. In fact, they constitute the oldest ethnic group in the county, and were in a majority only 150 years ago. During the 18th and 19th centuries many Finns from neighbouring Finland settled in these parts. To-day the racial distinctions between the various groups are so blurred that it is no longer possible to keep accurate statistics. In 1950 12.3% used Lappish as their daily speech, 2.5% Finnish, and 1.7% two languages. During the last 35 years Norwegian has tended more and more to oust these languages. Today there are no nomadic Lapps, although some 1600 of them still depend for their livelihood on their herds of tame reindeeer. They spend the winter in permanent houses on the plateau, herding their animals with the aid of motor-scooters, in spring they move off towards the coast, and in autumn trek back to their home on the mountain moors. It is among these inhabitants of Finnmark that the typical and picturesque culture, traditions and language of the Lapps will survive longest.

A feature of Finnmark is the marked difference in climate between the coastal and inland areas, between summer and winter. In summer it is cooler along the coast than inland, in winter the reverse is true. The coastal areas enjoy a more even temperature all the year round, while the difference between winter and summer temperatures in the interior is extreme. In Karasjok, for instance, the mercury often drops to 50 below (Centigrade), while summer temperatures of thirty-two degrees have been recorded. On the Finnmark plateau winter accounts for 210 days, and summer a mere 70 days of the year, viz. from about June 16 to August 23. Not until early July does the hawthorn flower in Kautokeino.

Havøysund

Meanwhile the coastal steamer has sailed through Rolvsøysund en route for Havøysund. *Havøysund* with approximately 1,700 inhabitants is the centre of the Måsøy community. Fishing is rich in the Arctic Ocean off the village, and there is no problem in supplying the processing plants. Before the North Cape road opens every spring, and if there is time to spare, the coastal steamer will round North Cape; the regular route goes through the Magerøy Sound to Honningsvåg.

We are rubbing shoulders with aristocratic ghosts in these waters, for on our left we can see Måsøy, where Louis Phillipe of Orleans, later renowned as the bourgeois king of France, stayed as the guest of the merchant Buch in 1795, during his trip to North Cape. The exiled Louis Philippe feared an attempt on his life, and for that reason travelled to these remote parts. He was one of the first tourists to visit North Cape. From Finnmark he made his way to North Sweden, where in a little Lapp village he had an affair with a clergyman's sister, who presented him with a blue-blooded offshoot of the Bourbons. Louis Philippe never forgot the hospitality he had received in Finnmark, and after he had become king of France, he sent in 1838 the frigate Recherche north with a bust of himself, twice life size. The people of Måsøy, however, had in the meantime moved to Havøysund, and here the bust stayed in the

54

best parlour of the merchant Rasch until the Germans burnt the village during the last war. A copy now stands at North Cape. The Norwegian painter, Balke, who resided in Paris from 1846 to 1847, received over 30 commissions from Louis Philippe, including a painting of the king at North Cape with the Arctic Ocean in the background. The church at Måsøy has led a restless existence: in 1746 it moved to Måsøy together with the vicar of Ingøy, but in 1832 the authorities decided that it ought to stand at Havøysund and finally in 1865 it was decided that it should stand at Måsøy, where also the hymn writer M. B. Landstad was born in 1802.

Through the narrow Magerøy Sound the costal express sails towards Honningsvåg. Every spring the reindeer of the Karasjok Lapps are ferried across the Magerøy Sound by one of the Navy's landing craft, as the calves are too small and weak as yet to tackle the swim across to their summer pastures. But in autumn, when the Karasjok Lapps start their trek back to the mountain moors, all the animals swim over to the mainland.

Honningsvåg with its 4,600 inhabitants is the largest fishing village **Honningsvåg** in West Finnmark. In earlier years Kjelvik was more important, but the old story was repeated: Honningsvåg had better harbour facilities, and so in the 1880's it became the senior partner. In 1882 the church at Kjelvik was actually blown into the sea, and the church which was to replace it was built at Honningsvåg. Hammerfest merchants set up branches in Honningsvåg, the first export trade was started, and the place grew. During the German retreat from the Murmansk front in 1944 Honningsvåg suffered the same fate as the rest of Finnmark, and was razed to the ground; only the church remained. Honningsvåg has been re-built and has found its proper place in the economic set-up of this part of the country. The town possesses one of Norway's busiest harbours, with four to five thousand ships calling per annum, the bulk of them trawlers, who take on their pilots at Honningsvåg. This is the home port of a large number of fishing vessels, and the harbour is ringed with fish-processing factories, producing numerous products, such as capelan oil and capelan meal, as well as yards, bunkering stations, and other institutions serving the needs of the fishing fleet. The biggest fish-processing firm, the Fi-No-Tro (Finnmark-Nord-Troms) plant processes fish, with deep-frozen fillets as its main product. The large building out on the spit of land is the State Fishery School.

In the past the coastal express used to anchor up in the little Hornvika bay at the foot of North Cape, while passengers were forced to scramble up to the top of this steep headland. To-day passengers go by bus from Honningsvåg to North Cape. It is a drive through typical tundra country. From Skipsfjordfjell the white

Honningsvåg is the largest fishing village in West Finnmark, as a harbour full of fishing smacks and a sky dotted with questing seagulls attest.

In the background North Cape with its characteristic horn. In the foreground Skarsvåg, the most northerly inhabited spot in Norway

shape of mount Duken, renowned for its rare flora, can be seen to the north-east. Here are to be found species that are otherwise only to be seen in Spitzbergen or Novaya Semlja. Some of them probably survived the last Ice Age, and may therefore be classed with Norway's interglacial flora. To the north can now be seen North Cape with its characteristic "horn". Herds of reindeer are a common sight along the road. Though Magerøya literally means "meagre island", Lapp families from Karasjok pasture as many as 4,000 reindeer here, and there is no difficulty in finding ample summer grazing.

North Cape Before the ascent to the *North Cape* plateau starts a side road takes off to Skarsvaag, the most northerly inhabited place in the whole of Norway and the world's northernmost fishing village, with a population of 225.

On the North Cape plateau stands a monument commemorating the visit of King Oscar II in 1873. The king's journey was widely published, and more than any other event helped to stimulate travel to the Land of the Midnight Sun. A few years after the royal visit coastal vessels made regular trips to North Cape, where, at 71° 10' 21" latitude north, the whole disc of the Midnight Sun is visible from 14th May to 30th July. "If we take into account the total sum of light provided by this day of 1,440 hours duration, the twilight, the northern lights, the moonlight and starlight, we get more light than is enjoyed by residing on the Equator", the Reverend Deinboll, who had made very accurate observations, once wrote.

Outside the North Cape Hall there is a bust of another famous visitor, Louis Philippe of Orleans, king of France 1830–48. The statue of the Virgin Mary and the Infant Jesus was erected with funds collected by school children in the Italian town of Modena, at the suggestion of a teacher and botanist by the name of Tino Zuccoli who published in 1973 in Bologna a work entitled *Flora Arctica*, dealing with plants growing north of the Arctic Circle. All flora and fauna on the North Cape plateau, on the slopes running down to Hornvika and in Hornvika itself, are protected. In the Hall special North Cape stamps are on sale and postcards and letters can be franked and sent from here.

It was the English explorer Richard Chancellor who gave it the name North Cape, when during an attempt to discover the North-East Passage in 1553 he drifted along the Norwegian coast. The Englishman failed to discover a sea route to India, but these bold merchant adventurers started a flourishing trade with the Murmansk coast, which resulted, among other things, in the growth of Archangel. For many years England and the dual Dano-Norwegian monarchy disputed the sovereignty of these northern waters, until England in 1583 recognized the rights of the King of Norway and Denmark, and the Muscovy Company agreed to pay an annual rate for the right to sail in these waters. In more recent times another English sailor, after sending the German battle-ship Scharnhorst to the bottom off the coast of Finnmark on December 20, 1943 was created Lord Frazer of North Cape. From the spring of 1943 this ship and the *Tirpitz* had been based in North Norway, operating against Allied convoys sailing to Russia. To protect this shipping strong naval escorts had to be made available. It was the battleship *Duke of York* assisted by a cruiser and four destroyers — one of them the Norwegian *Stord* — that surprised and sank the *Scharnhorst* after an engagement lasting several hours. Out of a crew of 1,970 only 36 were saved.

The cliffs between Porsanger and Laksefjord are called *Sværholt-klubben*, and are considered to constitute one of Norway's largest bird rocks. The birds nesting here are mostly kittiwakes and terns. In the olden days as many as 10,000 eggs were collected here for preservation. It is not unusual to see a sea eagle hovering over Sværholtklubben. Round the "corner" once stood the exposed fishing village of Sværholt. A previous owner of the village and two of his brothers were drowned one stormy day when they were trying to transfer to the local steamer, a tragic event similar to hundreds up and down the coast of Finnmark. **Sværholt-klubben**

All the coastal steamers call at Kjøllefjord, while the other fishing villages on the Nordkyn peninsula, Mehamn and Gamvik, have fewer calls. Sailing into *Kjøllefjord,* we can see *Finnkjerka,* a set of peculiar weathered stones and said to be the most graceful sea-cliff in Norway. It was not climbed until 1955. *Kapellet,* the Chapel, another sea-cliff close by, is unclimbed. There is a beacon light standing at Galgeneset or Gallows Point, a reminder of the fact that at one time Finnmark was a place of exile for convicts. The unusual Kjøllefjord church is a gift from Danish parishes. The next inlet on the Nordkyn peninsula is called the Oks Fjord. At its head grows the Oksvaag Forest, a natural birch forest, and — not surprisingly — the most northerly forest in the world. Fronting the open sea we catch sight of the tiny fishing community of Skjøtningberg. The rocky promontory east of the village, Smørbringa, is one of Finnmark's many bird rocks. The northernmost point on the peninsula of Nordkyn, *Kinnarodden,* is also the most northerly point on the European mainland, and lies at 71° 8′ North. Here we sail out across *Austhavet,* the last and longest of the open stretches on our trip. **Kjøllefjord** **Finnkjerka** **Kinnarodden** **Austhavet**

Mehamn, where four coastal steamers call, is one of the more recently built fishing villages in Finnmark. It was here that 1,500 fishermen in 1903 staged an attack on the whaling station, because their demands that the whale should be preserved had been turned down. The fishermen believed in fact that it was the whale which drove the shoals of capelan (a little fish on which the cod feeds) **Mehamn**

At the entrance to Kjøllefjord will be seen a rock known locally as the Finn Church, with the Chapel close by.

towards the coast, and for that reason they were very keen to preserve the whale. By the time the whale was placed on the list of protected animals (the year after) it was almost extinct in these waters. Nevertheless there was plenty of cod both in 1904 and 1905, whatever the reason for this may have been. Mehamn has an airport, the most northerly on the European mainland to be served by scheduled flights.

Bispen At Kamøy light we catch sight of *Bispen* (The Bishop), a peculiar rock formation amazingly like a clergyman standing in his pulpit.

Gamvik Before reaching *Gamvik*, we pass the world's northernmost light-

Kinnarodden, the northernmost point on the European mainland, is a steep promontory scored with deep clefts.

house at Slettnes. The coastal express does not come alongside at Gamvik: passengers and freight are ferried ashore in lighters, a tricky operation in the dark when there's a sea running. Before we set a course across the mouth of the Tana Fjord we pass yet another bird rock, the Omgangsstauran, on the eastern point of the Nordkyn peninsula.

On the northwest corner of the Varanger Peninsula we shall spot the steep conical shape of Tanahorn, a well-known landmark some 850 ft. high, and once a Lapp place of sacrifice. At *Berlevåg* too **Berlevåg** passengers had to be transferred from the steamer to an open boat in order to land, but in 1975 work on the breakwaters had proceeded so far that coastal steamers could make regular calls. This was no easy task. On two occasions the breakwaters were smashed by the fury of the storm. A solution was found in the use of tetrapods, huge interlocking concrete blocks, the smallest of which weigh 15 tons, while the biggest, covering the head of the breakwater, weigh 25 tons. Waves over 30 ft. high have since been recorded but the structure has withstood the assault. This was a highly necessary precaution, in the light of previous experience. In 1882 a storm swept across Berlevåg, sending all the fishingboats to the bottom, and a similar disaster occurred in our own century. Today the fleet lies secure in the lee of the breakwater, ensuring a livelihood for 1,700 persons who work as fishermen or in fish-processing factories. Berlevaag also has an airport with regular departure and arrivals. For a good many years Berlevåg has been linked by road — in summer only — to the North Norway highway.

The stretch from Berlevåg to Kirkenes is described under day 7.

SEVENTH DAY:

Kirkenes to Båtsfjord

We have now reached the turning point in our journey, the town **Kirkenes** of *Kirkenes* near the mouth of the Pasvik river. Kirkenes has 5,000 inhabitants, and the history of this township is closely bound up with that of the Syd-Varanger Company, Norway's largest mining concern, which was started in 1906, and whose iron ore mines are situated at Bjørnevatn, 7 miles from Kirkenes.

On October 25th, 1944, the Russians liberated Kirkenes, but not before the Germans had succeeded in destroying most of the town and damaging the mining plant. During the fighting around Kirkenes several thousand people took refuge in the mines at Bjørnevatn. Many lived there for weeks, and ten children were born in the underground passages. After the war the work of rebuilding commenced with the State as chief shareholder in the mining company, which yields some 6 million tons of ore annually, and employs 1,250 people. Strenuous efforts are being made to improve operating results. Closing down the plant would literally mean the complete depopulation of Kirkenes, a solution no government could accept.

The green and wooded Pasvik valley, which provides Kirkenes with produce, was first farmed by Finnish settlers who moved in from the south. In 1870 farmers from South Norway "colonized" this district, but it was not till good roads were built in the present century that a large-scale influx started. Before the war traffic passed unhampered across the Pasvik river to Finland, but now that the Petsamo area has become Russian territory, an invisible barrier has been raised along the river line. From the Jarfjord road on the other side of the bridge across the Pasvik river it is possible to look through the Iron Curtain at Boris Gleb, but cameras and field glasses are strictly taboo at the border.

Some coastal express ships call at *Vadsø* on the northbound trip, **Vadsø** most of them in the morning on the southbound trip. Vadsø (pop. 5,800) is the administrative centre of Finnmark. This town contains not only the residence of the County Sheriff, but also the County Surveyor of Roads, and the Finnmark Radio Station. The original fishing village was situated on the island of Vadsøy, but in 1710 the church was moved to the mainland, and a community soon sprang up. It was not until 1833 that Vadsø acquired the rights and privileges of a township. At one time the Finnish settlers were in the majority: in 1875 62% of the population were Finnish-speaking, but today very little Finnish is heard in the streets of the town. Vadsø was subjected to continual Russian bomber attacks during the last war. One of the most destructive of these raids was the attack on August 23, 1944, when the centre of the town was burnt out. Part of the town was also burnt when the Germans retreated in October 1944.

One of the most remarkable events near Vadsø is the capelan fishing. Every year in February—April the capelan, a small herring-like fish of the salmon family, makes its way from the Arctic to spawning grounds off the coast of Finnmark. Vadsø is the centre of the capelan fisheries. Sometimes schools of these fish have made their way right into the harbour, where local fishermen have netted them practically in the heart of town. The last time this happened was ten years ago. The capelan is used as bait for the Lofoten and Finnmark fisheries, but the bulk goes to the capelan-oil-factories. The Finnmark fishing season, when cod is caught, takes place from the end of March to the beginning of June, and is one of Norway's largest seasonal fisheries.

The local economy is based on fishing. Only a relatively small percentage of the population gain their livelihood on the fishing banks, while the majority are employed in various forms of fish-processing, such as the production of capelan oil at Europe's biggest factory in that line, in canning, etc. Some fifty local farms provide work on the land, but public administration even so accounts for the largest number of work places, followed by business activities and the service trades. These last three categories together employ about one half the working population. The island of Vadsøya, where the original town stood, is incidentally enjoying

On the "green side" of the Varanger peninsula stands the town of Vadsø.

Vardø with Vardøhus Fortress in the foreground, the coastal express in the middle of the picture and Hornøya, Norway's easternmost point, in the background.

quite a renaissance, with the capelan oil factory and a deep-water quay, where the coastal express berths. There is an ebb and flow at neeps and full moon with a difference of as much as 4 metres, not much by English standards but quite considerable for Norway.

At Vadsøya, too, may be seen the mast to which Roald Amundsen's airship Norge was moored in 1926, and which was later used by Umberto Nobile for his airship Italia in 1928. Here too may be seen medieval sites — including a churchyard — which testify to the age of the town. A stone's throw from Vadsø church, which is open all through the summer, stands the Immigrant Monument, the work of the Finnish sculptor Ensio Säppänen. Unveiled in the summer of 1977 in the presence of the President of Finland and the Kings of Sweden and Norway, it commemorates the large-scale immigration of Finns to Finnmark in the 19th century.

Skirting the "green" side of the Varanger peninsula our ship heads for Vardø. Out at sea the fishing fleet can often be seen in operation, while on land fishing villages big and small can be picked out. First comes Ekkerøy, where Viking Age graves have been discovered, probably deriving from a trading post far north of permanent Norwegian habitations. The bird colony on Ekkerøy is the home of kittiwake, black-backed gulls, auk and many other varities. The next two fishing communities, Skallelv and Komagvær, have opted for harbours at the mouths of rivers. In Skallelv Finnish is still spoken "in the home". Near Komagelv remains of massive German fortifications can still be seen. There were fortifications as well at Kibergnes, the easternmost point on the Norwegian mainland, and in the 127-metre-high Domen hill between Kiberg and Vardø. Domen was also supposed to have been a meeting place for witches at Christmas and Midsummer in days gone by.

Vardø   There has been talk of moving *Vardø* across to the mainland. This could have been done after the last war, when ⅔ of all houses lay in ruins, as a result of Russian bombing raids. However, Norway's most easterly town was rebuilt on the old site round South and North Våg. All the same, the plan to link Vardø to the mainland has been realized. Since 1984 it has been possible to drive beneath the waters of Bussesund to the mainland through Norway's first submarine road tunnel. Three km in length, it reaches its lowest point 88 m under the surface of the water.

At the end of the 13th century the Russians gained control of the Kola area, and the peninsula was henceforth closed to Norwegian fur-traders. The county of Finnmark was threatened, and in 1307 the first church was erected on the island of Vardø. The church, by carrying out missionary work among the Lapps, aimed to preserve

Norwegian influence in the border country. At about the same time the fortress of Vardøhus was built. Norwegian and Russian influence each gained the ascendancy in turn in disputed areas, even after the peace and boundary treaty in 1326 had established more settled conditions. As a rule the unfortunate Lapps were forced to pay taxes to both countries. All that is left of the original fortress is a beam on which King Christian IV wrote his name in 1599, King Oscar II in 1873, and on which King Haakon VII followed suit with his signature in 1907 and King Olav V in 1959. From 1734 to 1738 Christian V built the present Vardøhus fortress at Vestøy, in the shape of an octagonal star-shaped redoubt with four bastions. It was dismantled in 1792, but when the Russians shortly afterwards evinced an interest in Finnmark it was once more placed in a state of readiness. Today the fortress is open to tourists. Vardø's one and only tree can be seen here. This is a rowan near the Commandant's house, which is carefully cocooned every autumn to enable it to survive the winter. The first day when the entire disc of the sun is visible after two months of winter darkness a salute is fired from Vardøhus Fortress. This is usually about January 20. That day is also a whole holiday for all local school children.

At the time this part of Norway was called Vardøhus the town was really the capital of Finnmark. However, it did not acquire the rights of a township until 1789. After 1850 Vardø developed until it became Norway's largest fishing port, and trade with Russian was very lively. Before the first World War the Russians maintained during the summer months a combined passenger-and cargo route between Archangel and Vardø. Today Vardø has a population of 4,000, a large fishing-fleet and a corresponding fish processing industry. The Fi-No-Tro Plant includes a filleting plant, a refrigeration plant, installations for dried and salted fish, etc. Vardø has several private firms in the fish processing branch, as well as packaging capelan for the Japanese consumer market. The Vardøhus Museum has a number of interesting collections. The large tower-like building which is easily visible from the sea as we approach, is the town hall. Vardø church from 1958 is open when the Coastal Steamer calls.

The little island of Hornøya north of the town is Norway's easternmost point, lying 31° 10′ 4″ East of Greenwich. On the island, which also includes a bird rock, stands Vardø lighthouse. With an illumination of 2 million candlepower it can be seen 23 nautical miles away.

We have already seen that the Russian business men who came to Finnmark before the first World War were always welcomed by the population. Hundreds of Russian coasting smacks, with their goodnatured skippers and peasants from the White Sea, would sail into the fishing villages of Finnmark to barter flour and grain, which had been ferried down the Dvina on large rafts, for fish. The people of Finnmark welcomed this barter trade for two reasons. First of all they were sorely in need of the goods the Russians brought with them, and secondly they got rid of fish which could not keep hanging out to dry in the summer owing to the danger of maggots. The established form of barter was a measure (40 lb) of wheat for 3 measures of coalfish or cod. The language used by these traders was a curious mixture of Norwegian, Russian, Dutch and English, and both parties were confident that they were really fluent in the language of their opposite number. The prime reason for this barter trade was the great need for fish during the many fasts which the Russian observed.

We are now out on the Austhavet, shaping a course for Båtsfjord. To landward we have Norway's largest and most barren peninsula, the Varanger Peninsula. In some places weathering has stripped the ground of every vestige of vegetation, but there are extensive stretches of reindeer-moss, where herds find pasture in summer. From the deck of your steamer you can see the rugged, broken face the peninsula turns to the open sea: cliffs and rocks twisted into weird shapes by the elements, moulded into the semblance of turrets, spires and battlements.

About half way beween Vardø and Båtsfjord we pass the Syltefjord. On the north side of the fjord, not far from its outlet, can **Syltefjord-** be seen *Syltefjordstauran*, one of Norway's largest bird-rocks. Mile **stauren** upon of its beetling cliffs are covered with nests. Syltefjordstauran is dominated by kittiwakes. Estimates of their number cary from 300,000 to 3 million. But it is no easy task counting birds on the wing. One of the prominent rocks on this cliff face is Storalke-stauren (lit. the great auk pillar), not least now that it is the home of a colony of the rare stormy petrel. The fulmar is another rare species, while the king auk is said to have its only European nesting site on this bird-rock.

Båtsfjord *Båtsfjord* is an old fishing village. After it had become a port of call for the coastal steamer, a rapid development took place. Båtsfjord, relatively undamaged in the last war, acted as the main supply centre for North Norway after Finnmark had been liberated. Subsequently Båtsfjord has expanded rapidly, and is to-day Norway's "largest" fishing village, in terms of volume of catch.It has a population of some 3,000, of whom 250 net the fish on which Båtsfjord lives. Twice as many work in the refrigerator plant, the filleting factory, the capelan oil factory, the train oil plant, and the ship repair yards. The curious stripes in the cliffs at Båtsfjord are due to sedimentation, and movements in the earth's crust explain why they run at an angle to the horizontal.

The stretch Berlevåg to Hammerfest is described under day 6.

The stretch from the arctic circle to East Finnmark might well be called the bird rock run. Our picture shows Syltefjordstauran, one of the bird rocks of Finnmark.

Hammerfest to Skjervøy

Hammerfest *Hammerfest,* with its 7,500 inhabitants, lies at the foot of Mount Salen. Some scholars believe that the name of the town indicates that it is securely fastened (*fest* means to fasten) to Salen, which at times provides an insecure foothold. Avalanches from the mountain have swept away houses as well as people. Hammerfest is the world's northernmost town, its exact latitude being 70° 39′ 48″ latitude north, a figure which, apart from a devitation of one minute, is inscribed on the memorial set up at Fuglenes to commemorate the geodetic survey work which Russia, Sweden and Norway undertook jointly from 1819 to 1852, with the object of determining the shape and size of the world. In the world's northernmost town the summer day lasts from 17th May to 28th July, and there is darkness from 21st November to 23rd January. In order to lighten the darkness Hammerfest procured the first municipal power station in Norway as early as 1891.

Down through the ages Hammerfest was an established trading centre because it possessed the best winter harbour in Finnmark. In conjunction with the easing of trade restrictions it acquired the privileges of a township in 1789. Despite the fact that all who settled in the town were exempt from taxation, to start with there were only 40 inhabitants, but 23 years later the population figures had reached 350. Already in 1789 Consul Buch had fitted out the first expedition to winter in Svalbard, thus providing an important basis for the town's further development. The trade with the Russians and fishing were other growth factors.

During the Napoleonic wars when Finnmark was cut off from supplies from the South, imports of Russian corn were indispensable to this part of Norway. The English sent naval units to Finnmark to put an end to this grain trade, and in 1809 the brigs "Snake" and "Fancy" bombarded Hammerfest. The citizens of Hammerfest replied as well as they could with the small guns in the batteries at Fuglenes and Batteribakken.

When regular sailings to the North Cape were started in earnest, the tourist trade became a good source of income to the town.

During the last war the Germans used Hammerfest as a naval base. In October 1944 the Germans forcibly evacuated all the inhabitants and razed the town to the ground. This was not the first time: in 1891 a fire had reduced the town to a heap of ashes. This stubborn urge to build a home and live up here in the remote north might seem surprising, but in time the world's northernmost town was rebuilt for the second time in fifty years. The boldest and most attractive architecture in town is the label generally given to the new church, where the entire east wall is in the form a single stained glass window, vibrant with glowing colours. St. Michael's Church was consecrated in 1958. It was built by German catholic volunteers. The mosaic work on the facade, depicting St. Michael and the dragon, consists of 10,000 pieces. Another attraction is the little museum in the town hall, the collections of the Polar Bear Club, telling the story of Hammerfest's traditions as a trapping and arctic centre.

In every way the bustling life round the harbour shows that this is one of the largest fishing towns on this coast. The Findus fish-processing plant, with deep-frozen fillets as its speciality, is the most important local concern, employing nearly 1,000 persons on shore and onboard a fleet of trawlers. The Hammerfest district has more than 1,000 fishermen, a number that exceeds those employed in industry. In Hammerfest, too, are the head offices of The Finnmark County Steamship and Bus Co. With its local steamers, ferries and buses this company serves Norway's largest county, and what is undoubtedly one of Europe's most difficult traffic areas. For this reason transport by land and sea provide employment for many. A stroll through the streets shows that trade and commerce cover a wide range. The latest venture is oil: situated close to the Tromsøflak banks where prospecting is going on, Hammerfest is a natural choice as a base, and is a much frequented port-of-call for supply ships. The search for oil and gas has produced many spin-offs locally. The health service, hotels, laundries, workshops, contractors, the harbour authorities, transport companies and bunkering facilities are all favourably affected. Hammerfest's feeder airport, more in demand than any other feeder airport in Norway, is now too small.

Sørøya, Norway's fourth largest island to the west of Hammerfest, **Sørøya** was the scene of dramatic events during the last war. 1,000 people, defying the German orders for a mass evacuation, managed to conceal themselves in the caves in the mountains. Their situation was eventually desperate, and 200 were under conditions of extreme danger transferred to Båtsfjord in liberated Norway, while the remainder were picked up by destroyers attached to a Murmansk convoy and brought to Glasgow in January 1945. Some coastal express steamers call at the village of *Hasvik* in the far south of the **Hasvik** island. Here the Dutch ran a whaling station in the 17th century. From Hasvik there is a road to Breivikbotn and Sørvær, and consequently a considerable amount of freight is off-loaded on the quay at Hasvik, where salt fish, dried fish and klip fish are also produced and fresh fish exported on the coastal express.

The coastal express ploughs on down Sørøy Sound. On the left

Hammerfest owes its growth to the possession of the best winter harbour in Finnmark. Today this, the world's northernmost town, has a population of 7,500.

lies Seiland, with the Nordmannsjøkulen (3,500 ft.) and Seilandsjøkulen (3,200 ft.), Norway's eighth largest island. Further down the coastal leads we shall have Stjernøya to port. Here a rare mineral, nephelin-syenite, is quarried for the manufacture of porcelain. On the islands of Sørøya, Seiland and Stjernøya the Kautokeino Lapps pasture their reindeer in summer.

Øksfjord   *Øksfjord*, at which all ships of the coastal express service call, has been the scene of lively trading activity ever since 1818. The annual herring fisheries in the fjord just off Øksfjord assured its existence and provided the raw materials for the herring oil factory "Njord"

The Øksfjordjøkul is the only glacier in the Norway that calves straight into the sea, making it possible for fishermen in the Jøkel Fjord to get their ice from the sea for free.

which now mainly processes capelan into oil and meal. And if no capelan is available fillets, train oil and fishmeal are produced. This factory was put out of use by a Norwegian raiding party on April 12th, 1941, onboard the destroyer "Mansfield", commanded by Captain Ulstrup, Royal Norwegian Navy. The glacier visible on the other side of the fjord is the Øksfjordjøkulen (3,800 ft. above sea level), Norway's fifth largest glacier, the only one to calve into the sea, a phenomenon that can be observed in the Jøkel Fjord in Kvænangen.

The locality hardly breathes an air of romance, and yet romance is a flower that blossoms in the loneliest of fishing villages. Once upon a time there was a girl from Øksfjord called Philippa Schwensen. Just before her . 17th birthday, she met an English naval officer, George Temple, who was visiting Finnmark in his yacht. They fell in love and became engaged, but he had to return home, and he was absent for five long years. His parents were against the union, but their love endured, and after five years' absence he returned to fetch his beloved Philippa and return with her to England, where she made a great hit in London society. This story would have been forgotten had not the authoress Marie Corelli come across it during a journey to North Cape, and used it for her best-selling novel entitled "Thelma" or "The Norwegian Princess".

Loppa The fifth of the open stretches of sea on our journey—Lopphavet — is named after the tiny island of *Loppa* (The Flea), which round about the year 1860 was visited by English sportsmen. A certain Mr. White, who was anxious to rent the shooting rights, applied to a lawyer in Tromsø. The lawyer's English was not particulary good, and owing to a mistake he drew up a deed of sale, whereby the Englishman purchased Loppa for 2,000 dollars. Loppa had a number of English owners before it once more became Norwegian property in 1890.

Skjervøy In the evening we approach *Skjervøy*, a village with a backdrop of mountain peaks unmatched on our voyage. Finds indicate that people have lived here ever since the Stone Age. Skjervøy is very favourably placed on the direct sea-lanes between Troms and Finnmark, and possesses venerable traditions as a trading post. In the 17th century Christen Michelsen Heggelund, nicknamed the King of Skjervøy, was the leading local personality. This colourful merchant was known for his high-handed business methods. He even helped himself to the church offertory plate to recoup a debt owed him by the vicar, and not surprisingly has found a niche in the poems of Petter Dass, the clergyman who wrote so amusingly of this little-known part of Norway. The remains of the Swedish Arctic explorers Andrée and Strindberg were brought in to Skjervøy in 1930, and it was here that Otto Sverdrup arrived in August 1896 with the "Fram" after long years in the Arctic. Skjervøy is to-day the largest fishing village in North-Troms with a population of close on 2,500, of whom some 500 are actively engaged in fishing. About the same number work in filleting factories or in packaging shrimps or at the ship-building yard.

The stretch from Lyngstua to Harstad is described under day 5.

Harstad to Raftsund

Southbound an overland trip from Harstad to Sortland is arranged. The excursion frequently includes a visit to the new church in Harstad and to the old medieval church at Trondenes.

Between Andøya and Hinnøya runs the Risøy channel, $2\frac{3}{4}$ miles long and at one time silted up. The cost of dredging came to 4 million kroner, and was finally completed in 1922 when King Haakon VII attended the opening ceremony. Previously the coastal express steamers had passed through Tjeldsund Sound. Now Vesterålen enjoyed the benefit of the most important means of communication along the coast. It is no exaggeration to say that coastal express steamers opened up a new era for these islands. Outside Andøya the fishing banks come closer to the shore than they do anywhere along this coast, and the enterprising fishing villages of Bleik, Andenes and Dverberg reap a rich harvest in these waters. The fish is transported by truck to *Risøyhamn*, and is then **Risøyhamn** shipped on the coastal express. In this little coastal settlement and communication centre trade has been carried on for over 200 years.

Vesterålen (ålen = ocean) is more luxuriant than the Lofotens, and on the broad coastal fringe farms are thickly clustered in little rural communities which run in a continuous chain. On the flat Island of Andøya we find Norway's largest bog, nearly 25,000 acres in extent, and containing large areas of arable land. This gives the island in some respects the appearance of a vast aircraft-carrier with superstructure. In the far north of the island is an airport which, with its staff of 250, is the biggest employer of labour locally. In other respects Andøya is known to possess sources of coal — not commercially viable — from the Jurassic period. There are also numerous strata of remains from human habitation in the Middle Ages. The fishing communities at Andenes and Bleik are built on strata of this kind, in some cases 20 ft. deep. Andøya also contains Iron Age sites, burial mounds and graves from the Viking Age.

A new era to is being opened up by the Vesterålen bridges which link the islands to the mainland. At Risøyhamn we pass under the 750-metre-long Andøy bridge. Before Sortland we observe the 425 metre-long Kvalsauken bridge that spans the Hognfjord. These bridges were completed in 1974. At Sortland we glide under the 961-metre-long Sortland bridge, completed 1975, and between Langøya and Stokmarknes the last of these bridges, 1,020 metres long Hadsel bridge, was opened in 1978. This bridge is fitted with a high-frequency sonic device to prevent foxes crossing over to Hadseløya, as they did to Andøya when the Andøy bridge was completed.

When the coastal express passes through the narrow Risøyrenna between Andøya and Hinnøya the sandy bottom can be seen through the water on both sides. This channel needs constant dredging to ensure that there's enough water under the keel.

Sortland   *Sortland*, with its 3,100 inhabitants, is known to us from saga times. It was here that the brothers Karle and Gunnstein, who accompanied Tore Hund on his journey to Bjarmeland, lived in the 11th century. Sortland farm has ever since 1781 belonged to the Ellingsen family, who are descended from the Benkestoks.

Sortland is the communication centre of Vesterålen, and the main base for the Norwegian Navy's coastal guard vessels. It also has a canning factory, dairy and slaughterhouse, as well as a

The Sortland Bridge is one of a chain of five linking Vesterålen with the mainland. It has a main span of 150 m, and a clear height of 30 m.

company operating fishing smacks. While the coastal express passes down the Sortland Sound between Hinnøya, Norway's largest island, to port, and Langøya, the third largest, to starboard, wonderful views of Hinnøya and the white Møysalen peak (4,200 ft.) are enjoyed.

The flat coastal strip on Langøya has yielded finds from the Viking Age. Farms with names such as *Hov* (pagan temple), *Bø* (dwellingplace, farm) and *Vik* (creek) are among the oldest known to us. Non-compound names of this kind usually go back beyond the Viking Age, frequently to the late Iron Age, (c. 500 BC — c. 400

AD). Skagen, on which Stokmarknes airport is situated, means "headland". In 1980 some 55,000 passengers landed or took off here, making it Number 2 feeder airport in Norway.

Stokmarknes *Stokmarknes* (population 3,000) had an annual market from 1851—1939. It was visited by men from Bindal and Rana who came with their boats and their wooden articles. Mountebanks would put up their tents and people make merry in the light summer evenings. These fairs provided a well-earned change from the darkness and toil of the winter nights, and their passing is to be regretted. (Other well-known fairs in Nordland were held at Tilrem near Brønnøysund, Bjørn on Dønna and Kabelvåg). Stokmarknes is the headquarters of the Vesteraalen Steamship Company, which was founded by Richard With, the father of the coastal express, in 1881. Richard With was subsequently head of this firm, which today possesses a fleet of 15 ships, four of which are on the coastal express route. Stokmarknes possesses North Norway's second largest merchant fleet, surpassed only by Tromsø, and there are courses in theory, seamanship and cooking for seamen at the local folk high school. Apart from the shipping company, the county hospital, with its nursing school, is the biggest employer of labour.

Raftsundet *Raftsund* is the name of the fairway that runs from Vesterålen to Lofoten, but before we get as far as this we have a chance of admiring the northern side of Lofotens, while we are still out in the Hadsel Fjord. Higrafstind, a peak 3,800 ft. high, and the highest in Lofotens, stands out from among the other tops. In the Raftsund we **Troll Fjord** make a detour into the unusually wild and desolate *Troll Fjord*. At its entrance the 2 km long fjord is only a hundred metres wide. From the head of the fjord a path leads up to Lake Trollvatn, 530 ft. above sea level, where floes of ice drift around even in the middle of the summer. South of the fjord the jagged Trolltind peaks cut the skyline. Sometimes shoals of Lofoten cod have lost their way up the Troll Fjord, and on these occasions the fishermen sometimes have made large catches, after blowing the ice with dynamite. In his novel "The last Viking" Johan Bojer gives a dramatic account of "The Battle of Trollfjord", in 1880, when there was a clash between fishermen in small boats and fishermen in steam vessels, after the latter had penned a huge shoal of fish in the fjord with their nets. Gunnar Berg's painting of the "Battle of Troll Fjord" hangs in the Town Hall at Svolvær.

Leaving the Raftsund we catch a glimpse of the Hamarøy mountains, with their characteristic peaks, to the south-east.

The stretch Raftsund to Hestmannøy is described under day 4.

TENTH DAY:

Hestmannøy to Torghatten

Hestmannen (The Horseman) is astern, and we are no more in the Land of the Midnight Sun. Lurøy, to the right, is owned by the Norwegian branch of the Scottish Dundas family. The father of Petter Dass, the poet, was the first Dundas to settle in Norway. Between Lurøy and Tomma we catch sight of the hatshaped cone of Lovunden, the resting place of thousands of puffins. Further out to sea to the northwest, in clear weather, we should also be able to see Træna, which is composed of 400 islands and reefs. The peculiar Trænstaven is 1,100 ft. high. Important archeological excavations have been made in Kirkhelleren at Sanda, one of the islands. Before Sandnessjøen the coastal steamer puts into *Nesna,* beautifully **Nesna** situated on the spit of land between the Sjona and Rana fjords, with direct road connection to Mo i Rana. On the southern spit of the little island of Løkta stands Kopardal, one of the trading centres in the old fairway.

Before reaching Sandnessjøen we have *Dønna* to the right, with **Dønna** Mount Dønmannen (2,600 ft) in the south and in the north Dønna manor, one of the few large farms in Norway which truly deserves the name of manor, because it was the seat of a nobleman. Dønnes is also the only manor in North Norway which can boast a more or less continuous history as an estate from the saga times and right up to the present. From the middle of the 18th century until 1916 Dønnes was the nucleus of the Coldevin estates, which consisted of many properties. Dønna Church, a stone church from the thirteenth century with secret passenges built into its walls, contains the mortuary chapel of the Coldevin family. During restoration work, completed in 1974 over 500 coins and fragments of coins were found, the oldest dating back to the time of King Håkon Håkonsson (1204–1263). Practically in the very centre of the island of Dønna lies Bjørn, where Norway's second largest fair took place in the nineteenth century, with as many as three thousand people coming from far and near to attend and 150 booths.

Sandnessjøen, on the northern tip of the island of Alsten, is a **Sandnessjøen** trading centre dating back to the 1600's which awoke to new life and prosperty with the inauguration of the coastal express service. Its name implies that it was the point of disembarkation for Sandnes, the old seat of the Viking chieftain Torolv Kveldulvsson, who collected the Lapp tax for Harald Hårfagre. The king seems to have thought that Torolv was getting too powerful, for one summer he made his way north and liquidated his recalcitrant subject as well as his farm. Sandnes Farm was subsequently the residence of

79

*In the Raftsund we make a detour into the Troll Fjord, where there is just room
to squeeze by.*

The Rødøy Lion straddles the channel like a sphinx, 440 m high. Its reddish colour derives from the ferrous serpentine rock of which the island is composed.

the local governor for several hundred years. For 600 years the church stood at Sandnes, until in 1767 it was moved to Sandnessjø- en. Sandnessjøen is an important traffic centre. The Helgeland Transport Company, with its car ferries and fast local steamers, ensures connections between the various outlying islands and the urban centres at Mo i Rana and Mosjøen inland. Sandnessjøen is an industrial centre on the make, enjoying the benefits of various public projects. One result of this has been the firm of Noroff A/S, engaged on construction work for the offshore oil industry. The

Høvding ship breakers firm is another well-known name in an area mainly comprising small firms. In Sandnessjøen and its surroundings jobs are fairly evenly distributed between farming, fishing, industry and construction on the one hand and various forms of trade, administration and services on the other. We are now incidentally in a farming area: one fifth of the local labour force of round 5,000 are employed in agriculture.

The Seven Sisters *"The Seven Sisters"* (De syv søstre) are the last of the "persons" of our myth whose acquaintance we make on our cruise. Let us present them in the order in which we meet them: Botnkrona (3,300 ft.), Grytfoten (3,300 ft.), Skjæringen (3,400 ft.), The Twins (3,250 and 3,200 ft.), Hvastind (3,300 ft.), and Stortind (3,000 ft.). The sisters owe their shape to the six glaciers which have lain between them. The granite rock has been left standing in ridges between the hollows scooped out by glacial action. But let the beautiful maidens speak for themselves. Close to the shore, about halfway between **Alstahaug** Sandnessjøen and *Alstahaug* yet another feeder airport can be seen, Sandnessjøen airport, where planes flying between Trondheim and Bodø touch down.

Along the Helgeland coast, we have ample opportunity to study the coastline, which has a low flat foreshore, abruptly terminated by mountains further back, and continuing beyond the coast, in a broad belt of low reefs and islands. This flat coastal strip is a characteristic feature of the Norwegian coast, and of great importance to the population, for it was here, on soil that was easy to till, that the early settlements were made. In the county of Nordland, the majority of the population live on this flat coastal strip, which, if we add the islands and holms, in some places reaches a width of 30 miles. Scientists are of the opinion that it was caused by the action of the waves on the shore, in combination with frost heaving in the Ice Ages.

In some places along the flat shore strange rock formations withstood the onslaughts of breakers and frost. Weird shapes such as the Horseman, the Seven Sisters, Torghatten and other acquaintances such as the Rødøy Lion, Lovunden and Trænstaven are hard rocks that survived the kneading of the elements.

On the southern point of the island of Alsten lies *Alstahaug* with its 12th century church. The memorial stone we can see from the sea commemorates the parson-poet Petter Dass, who lived here from 1689 to his death in 1708, and ruled, with all the authority of a petty kinglet, over his wide-spread parish. His living was actually one of the richest in Norway, comprising more land than any other parish in Helgeland. His parishioners in turn worshipped their imperious and jocular parson. Petter Dass has described this part of Norway in "Nordlands Trompet" (The Trumpet of Nordland) with a realism which raised him far above the mediocracy of contemporary poets. There are plans to restore Alstahaug vicarage (from 1650) as it was in the days when Peter Dass carried out his parochial duties as well as engaging in a great deal of profitable trade. The King's Grave at Skjeggeneset, 30 m in diametre and 8 m high, is probably the biggest burial cairn in Nordland. In a smaller grave nearby Bronze Age finds have been made.

Alsten is joined by road to *Tjøtta*, one of the oldest inhabited spots **Tjøtta** in Helgeland, where Hårek of Tjøtta lived in the Saga period. Hårek was a great chieftain, and was one of those who killed St. Olav. North of the manor a star-shaped barton (farm yard) has been discovered from the Viking Age comprising the sites of 12 houses, 25 burial mounds and the monolith known as *Lekamøyas spö (Griddle stick)*. The other three monoliths on Tjøtta are called "The Griddle", "The Rolling Pin", and "The Dough". All these are associated with the legendary Lekamøya, who was said to be baking bread at Tjøtta when Hestmannen (The Horseman) came a-courting. At his approach she fled, leaving her baking implements behind, hence the names of these imposing stones. From the middle of the 18th century and right up to 1929 the Brodtkorb family owned Tjøtta. In the 19th century their estate comprised between 2 and 3 hundred farms, and their hospitality was legendary. In 1929 Tjøtta was bought by the State as a sheep-breeding station, and the estate is still the largest farm in North Norway. Easily visible from the sea is also the memorial stone bearing the Soviet star, marking the resting place of 8,000 Soviet-Russian prisoners of war who died of starvation, cold and torture in North Norway during the last war. There is no cross in the cemetery, but simply name-plates flush with the earth. On the right side of the channel lies the wreck of the *Rigel*, sunk with Russian prisoners of war on board in the last war, by Allied planes who had no knowledge of this transport. This tragic event resulted in the death of 2578 persons, making it one of the world's major maritime disasters. By comparison the wreck of the Titanic in 1912 claimed a death roll of 1502.

Between Tjøtta and Brønnøysund the large island of Vega will be seen to starboard. On its south side Trolltind and Vegtind arch their granite backs, and on the north, where mica provides better soil, close on 2,000 people comprise the most densely populated rural area in North Norway. One third of all employed persons work in agriculture, while one fifth earn a living by fishing.

The township of *Brønnøysund*, thanks to its strategic position on **Brønnøy-** the coastal express route, and its excellent harbour, ousted the **sund** market centre of Tilrem to the north and the trading centre of Kvaløy to the south. Today Brønnøysund has some 3,500 inhabitants, and the pleasant town is a centre of trade and communications. The Torghatten Transport Company provides transport by

The coastal express steamer operates all the year round, and many tourists prefer the winter cruises. Not surprising when the "Seven Sisters" are arrayed in their bridal gowns.

land and sea to the surrounding districts. Near the town limestone caves have been found, containing Stone Age dwellings, and a 10-minute trip by car from the quay brings the visitors to a spot in the mountains where a profile of Roald Amundsen can be seen quite clearly. "A wonderful monument, carved by nature's handwork, of one of Norway's heroes, a bold and courageous explorer in whose steps we meekly follow", wrote the polar explorer Sir Herbert Wilkins in the year book of the local tourist association in 1928.

A 550 m long bridge across Brønnøysund has now been completed, and this provides access by car to the foot of Torghatten. From here a 30-minute walk brings you to the "hole". But we shall be making a different approach.

After leaving Brønnøysund the coastal steamer in fact makes a **Torghatten** detour to the west round *Torghatten* to enable passengers to look through the hole which Hestmannen made with his arrow. The scientists, as might be expected, have their own explanation of this

The hole-in-the-mountain at Torghatten is so spacious that a fully-rigged sloop could sail through if the cave were a little lower, in fact where it was situated in the distant past when erosion did its work.

phenomenon. The mountain it appears, has a geological fault which runs in the direction of the ocean, and at the time when the land was some 330 to 350 feet lower than it is now, the action of frost and sea eroded the pliable, striped granite, causing this hole. The people of Nordland used to say that a fully rigged yacht could have sailed through the Torghatt, and they were certainly right, as the hole is 175 yards long, from 80 to 115 ft. high, and 40 to 80 ft. wide.

The stretch from Leka to Trondheim is described under Day 3.

Trondheim to Kristiansund N.

Trondheim   *Trondheim* is Norway's third largest town with some 135,000 inhabitants living within the limits of the revised municipal boundaries, which gives the town an area of 130 square miles. Previous population figures were about 60,000. The incorporation in 1964 of adjoining rural districts has made the ancient town one of Norway's largest agricultural communities, embracing over 900 farms. The central portion of the town is the peninsula between the fjord and the Nid river, and it is here that we also find the oldest and most interesting buildings. Broad streets and low wooden buildings, narrow alleys, old-fashioned warehouses and a picturesque town bridge gives this section of the town both charm and elegance. On the hills around the town and the slopes that run down to the river, as well as on "the island", the more modern part of the town has grown up, and in both eastern and western sections we find new and old architecture blending happily.

In 997 Olav Trygvesson, according to the saga, built a royal manor and a church at Nidarnes, and he is therefore usually regarded as the founder of the town. However, there must have been the nucleus of a township around the mouth of the Nid River as early as Viking times, in connection with the councils that met at Øra and the earldom of Lade. The renown and growing power enjoyed by the martyr king Olav the Saint stimulated its growth, and right up to the 13th century Nidaros, as it was then called, was the most important residence of Norwegian monarchs. In 1152 it became the seat of the newly established archbishopric, and as a result it became the natural spiritual centre of the country. Pilgrims came from far and near to be healed of their diseases at the shrine of St. Olav in Nidaros. In 1535 the Reformation reached Norway, and the last Catholic archbishop was forced to leave the country. From now on the town undergoes a period of decline. During the wars against Sweden in the 17th century Trondheim was repeatedly ravaged, gradually a series of disastrous fires destroyed many of the mediaeval buildings, and the present town centre owes its appearance to the Luxemburger, Johan Caspar von Cicignon, who drew up a new plan, assisted by the Dutchman Anthony Coucheron, in harmony with the gridded design of the age, after the fire of 1681. The town they created between them is something quite special, since we here find every basic type of town planning. The gridded pattern is obvious, while the "free" approach can be seen in irregular, narrow alleys which grew up within the large square blocks. The grid is typical of the Renaissance, while the free approach bears all the hallmarks of the Middle Ages. The radial effect is best observed from a position in the market place, from which broad avenues run — Munkegaten (Monk Street) and Kongensgate (King's Street). The fourth basic principle to emerge is the axial approach, which aims to emphasise prominent buildings. This function is taken care of by Munkegaten, which emphasises the Cathedral to the south and, in an extension of this street, Munkholmen out in the fjord to the north.

Culturally the town had undergone a period of almost complete stagnation after the Reformation, but in the middle of the 18th century it quickened to new life, thanks to the newly formed Royal Norwegian Scientific Society. Norway's oldest newspaper was first published in Trondheim in 1767, and the first public theatre was started there in 1803, while Norway's oldest school, the Cathedral School, celebrated its 950-year jubilee in 1980. Once again Trondheim was Norway's acknowledged cultural centre, and in our own day the university, which comprises the Technical High School and the Teachers' High School with their institutes, has created an important academic milieu, with the study of oil as one of its latest additions.

The Nidaros Cathedral is Norway's proudest jewel, and the largest mediaeval building in Scandinavia. The building probably antedates the founding of the archiepiscopal see. It is believed to have been built over the tomb of St. Olav, and in pre-Reformation times was one of the major goals of European pilgrims. Building extended over a considerable period. The transepts are Norman in style, while the chancel and nave are predominantly Gothic. The most important work of construction may be assumed to have been concluded around 1320. The beautiful cathedral was not allowed to stand for long in its full glory. One fire after another damaged it, and when the period of national decline set in, it soon proved impossible to carry out repair work. At the Reformation all the magnificent inventory, the sacred vessels, the shrine of St. Olav, and the altars were either destroyed or sent to Denmark. It has been said of the Nidaros Cathedral that it reflects the story of Norway: it took shape and grew during Norway's period of greatness, fell into a decline when Norway lost her sovereignty, and was restored when she once more won her freedom and independence. When restoration commenced in 1869 the church was little more than a ruin. Restoration has now been practically completed, though a little work still remains to be done on the west facade with its wealth of magnificent figures. Seven kings and three queens have been crowned in the Nidaros Cathedral, and nine kings and most of the archbishops lie buried here.

There are a good many buildings from the Middle Ages in the old

In the centre of the picture can be seen the Nidaros Cathedral, Trondheim's leading attraction, Norway's proudest gem and the biggest medieval church in the North.

part of Trondheim. Close to the Nidaros Cathedral stands the archiepiscopal palace from the 12th century, at one time the residence of Norway's supreme spiritual lord, after the Reformation of the governor. Today it houses the Nordenfjell Army Museum. A third ecclesiastical relic is the Church of Our Lady *(Vår Frues Kirke)* from the 13th century. This old Gothic church was extended westward in the 1600's and a tower added in the 1700's.

Wandering down Munkegaten (Monk Street) with its poplars, we shall find many beautiful wooden buildings, built by the old merchant families. The story goes that at the end of the 18th century three Trondheim ladies competed to see who could build the most beautiful town house. The results, praiseworthy in every way, were Møllmannsgården, Hornemannsgården and Schøllergården. The first of these was unfortunately destroyed by fire, the second now houses the Trondheim Police while the third is Stiftsgården, designed in the rococo style in the 1770's, Norway's second largest wooden building, and used after 1815 as a royal residence whenever the King visits Trondheim.

Other memorable sights include the Kristiansten Fortress, which also bears the mark of Cicignon's architectural talent, Sverresborg, with the Trøndelag Folk Museum, the collection of antiquities belonging to the Scientific Society, the Permanent Collections of the Art Association, and the Nordenfjeldske Museum of Applied Art. No one should miss a visit to one of Scandinavia's most fascinating museums, the Musical History Museum at the Old Ringve Manor. This is Norway's only museum for musical instruments. Visitors are taken round the collections by guides, who not only explain but play instruments from different epochs and countries. Northbound an excursion is arranged to Ringve. Tordenskiold, Norway's colourful naval hero, spent his childhood at Ringve.

Few city centres can be more conveniently explored on foot, on one's own, than Trondheim's. There's so much to see in such a small space, and the street scene is a fascinating one. Why not start your tour from the coastal express, cross the Østrekanal (East Canal) bridge to Fjordgaten, and follow this to the right along the picturesque warehouses to the Fish Hall at Ravnkloa. Then proceed up Munkegaten past Stiftsgården, via the marketplace with its statue of Olav Trygvesson, which is also a giant sundial, to the Cathedral and the Archbishop's Palace. Stroll through alleys to the old town bridge and spend the rest of your time moving at your leisure through Kongensgate, Dronningensgate, Olav Trygvessons gate and the bustling pedestrian walkways with their picturesque markets which cross them.

Norway's first kings were quick to realize Trondheim's strategic position, and for this reason they made it the capital of Norway. Its key position makes Trondheim today one of Norway's most important communication centres. The Nordenfjeldske Steamship Company has its head office in the town, and 4 important railways radiate from Trondheim, which is also a nodal point for important road, sea and air routes. Trade and industry have flourished thanks to easy communications. Of these, trade speaks for itself as we walk down the broad streets of the business quarters, while industry includes a wide range of products, both for home consumption and export, the latter comprising papers, chilled fillets of fish, canned products and metal goods.

A more exact breakdown of statistics shows that of the close on 50,000 work places about 15,000 are accounted for by industry, building and construction, about 6,000 by transport, about 12,000 by trade and business and almost 16,000 by administration and services. Most of those in the last-mentioned category are involved in education and the health services. If Trondheim were to have a label, it would read: Educational and trading centre.

Agdenes The voyage down the Trondheim Fjord has been described under Third Day, and will not be repeated here. At the mouth of the fjord, however, your attention is directed to *Agdenes* fort, built 1895–1900, on either side of the water. The commandant's house is at Hasselvika on the east side. Inadequately manned in 1940, it was no match for a German naval force consisting of the Admiral Hipper and three destroyers, which forced the narrows after a brief exchange of fire. Just west of Agdenes Lighthouse are the remains of the pier and church constructed at the orders of King Øystein Magnusson (about 1088–1123). It was at this spot, called Hamm, that many pilgrims on their way to the Nidaros Cathedral went ashore, to avoid the strong currents in the fjord, continuing on foot across land to the Nidaros Cathedral.

Hitra We now continue south, down the leads, between *Hitra* to the north and the mainland. With its 226 square miles, Hitra is the seventh largest island in Norway, and the largest south of Vesterålen. Low and marshy in parts, its interior is practically uninhabited, while a number of fishing communities are scattered along the coast. In the 1970's, however, the breeding of salmon and sea trout became the most important source of income on Hitra and the neighbouring island of Frøya. Today there are over 40 salmon and sea trout farms here and 5 hatcheries. Together these cover almost 20% of all "home-grown" salmon and sea trout in the country. Most of it is exported. Chief attraction is provided by a large herd of red deer. The landscape seen from the sea has a grey and monotonous appearance, a far cry from what is generally to be found in Norway.

Smøla, the next large island on our right, is even flatter than

90

Hitra, with its highest point only a little over 200 ft. above sea-level. To the east the bluff shapes of Tustna and Stabben tower little short of 3,000 ft. high. Geologists explain the strange configurations **Smøla** of the land by explaining that a "fault" has taken place involving a gigantic fissure parallel with the coast, so that the islands in the west have sunk about 3,000 ft. compared with those in the east.

Out at sea we can catch a glimpse of the *Grip* light, whose beams light up several hundred reefs and islands, which lie almost hull down, and bear such strange names as "The Devil", "The Killer", and "The Priest". Grip was one of the most remarkable communiti- **Grip** es in Norway — 100 souls living in weatherbeaten houses round a tarred stave church. To-day Grip is a desolate place. The last islanders left it in 1974. The houses on Grip nestle round their 400-year-old church as though seeking protection from the supernatural powers which the sea represents. On many occasions the waves have swept clear across Grip — in 1640 and 1820 only the church was left standing.

The stretch Kristiansund—Måløy is described under Day 2.

TWELFTH DAY:

Måløy to Bergen

The Coastal Express has called at Måløy and now passes through the narrow Skatestraum.

From Skatestraumen, where the current may run at several knots, we make our way to Frøysjøen. At the head of the Nord-Gulen Fjord lies Svelgen, where the Bremanger factory, which possesses Europe's largest electric smelting furnace for the production of ferro-silicium, is situated. Before reaching Florø we shall see the crest of Batalden, 1,600 ft. high, to the west. This island was often used as a landmark for Norwegian MTB's and sub-chasers operating from the Shetlands during the war.

Florø *Florø* is the chief centre of outer Sunnfjord, Norway's westernmost town, and the only town in the county of Sogn og Fjordane. After merging with neighbouring districts it is now a sizeable community, 274 sq. miles in area, but with a modest population figure of 9,000, of whom some 5,000 live in the town itself. The name Florø was taken from a farm where the township was founded as recently as 1860. Those who planned this community intended herring fishing to provide the main livelihood, but the ways of the herring are unpredictable, and Florø has sensibly developed other less speculative industries. The largest is Ankerløkken shipyard, employing 500 hands, which builds ships and also manufactures industrial equipment, and is becoming increasingly involved in the North Sea oil industry: immediately west of the town lies the richest oil and gas field on the Norwegian continental shelf — Statfjord. Florø operates as the regional harbour for Statfjord.

South of Florø the coastal express sails between Askrova, to **Svanøy** starboard, and *Svanøy*, to port. The latter has been called the "pearl of Sunnfjord", thanks to its unusually luxuriant vegetation, which is due to a soil rich in lime. The holly-trees on the island rise over 50 ft., while pines with a circumference of 13 ft. are no rarity. To-day the old estate has been made a scientific foundation with the aim of preserving and make better use of the natural resources of the West Coast. The old manor has been restored and turned into a study and conference centre.

A glance to the north-west will reveal the characteristic shape of Kinneklova, a strange cleft in the mountain and a well-known **Kinn** landmark on the island of *Kinn*. On this island stands a romantic stone church from the Middle Ages, one of the oldest in West Norway, with a magnificently preserved interior.

Alden Another prominent rock, *Alden* or the Norwegian Horse, should now be visible to the south-west. The name needs no detailed

92

The archipelago north and west of Bergen is often called "the grey realm". But it has a number of exciting passages, like narrow alleys, such as Rogneværleia west of Mongstad.

explanation. Alden is also referred to as the Norwegian Lion or the Blue Man. The many names have been coined by fishermen and sailors who used this 1,600 ft. pinnacle as a landmark. Beyond Alden Værlandet can be seen, and furthest out are the 350 islands of the Bulandet archipelago. The Germans found it impossible to prevent Norwegian fishing smacks from making their way to and from Britain, through this maze of islands, with arms and saboteurs. The wrath of the Germans was vented on the civilian population, and the people of Bulandet were the victims of German punitive measures.

Norwegian torpedo-boats, operating from the Shetland, also inflicted severe losses on German shipping between Stad and Bergen in countless daring raids. MTB 345 was one of the unlucky **Ospa** ones. In 1943 it was surprised by German naval units near Ospa, on our starboard bow south of Bufjord—the seven survivors of the battle, all in uniform, were shot at Ulven near Bergen on July 3rd. As this was a genuine naval vessel, the episode resulted in the death sentence being passed on the German Commander-in-Chief in Norway, General Nikolaus von Falkenhorst, at a trial in Germany of war criminals. This was subsequently commuted to a term of imprisonment.

Our ship now heads for the Solund archipelago which is said to comprise some 1,700 islands. Between Rånøy and Husøy, two small islands of rough grey rock and stone, which are so typical of this **Steinsundet** coast, runs *Steinsundet,* and through this sound we make for the waters of Sognesjøen, the "entrance hall" to the great Sogne Fjord. In actual length, measured from Rutletangen to Skjolden, this fjord is over 100 miles long. As well as being the longest fjord in Scandinavia, the Sogne Fjord is also the deepest, with depths of as much as 660 fathoms. Sognesjøen forms a marked shelf which only admits the warmer surface water to the fjord within.

The Holmengrå lighthouse marks the northern extremity of **Øygarden** *Øygarden* — the Skerry guard, which is the name for a string of low and barren islands west of the lead to Bergen. The border between the counties of Sogn and Fjordane and Hordaland is passed at the entrance to the Fens Fjord. To the east lies Vardetangen, the westernmost point on the Norwegian mainland, 4° 56' 58". Here too we also catch a glimpse of Mongstad, the biggest oil refinery in Scandinavia producing some 4 million tons of various brands **Det naue** annually. "Det naue", a narrow sound whose name—derived from the Dutch "Het nauwe", meaning narrow—recalls the many merchant vessels from Holland that sailed in these waters in the 17th and 18th centuries.

Herdla The church at *Herdla* has had an eventful history. First mentioned in 1146, it was sacked by British naval units in 1655, pulled down in 1861, restored in 1935, and once again pulled down by the Germans during the Occupation. Herdla Manor was a royal demesne in the Middle Ages. Philip Arnesson (1207–1217), a pretender to the throne during the struggle for power that raged in the 13th century, had one of his strongholds here. So did the Germans during the last war. They constructed large defence works, as well as an aerodrome on this flat island. The church tower proved an obstacle to planes landing, and the church had to be pulled down. The entire population of the island was evacuated for the duration of the war.

On the other side of Herdla the *Hjelte Fjord* is visible. It was up this channel that the Vikings sailed when they shaped a course for Hjaltland, as the Shetlands were called. The Vikings occupied the Shetlands, in the 9th century, and these islands were in the possession of the Norwegian crown right down to 1469. Throughout the Middle Ages a brisk trade was carried on between Bergen and the Shetlands, as the name of the fjord suggests.

The approach to Bergen lies between Holsnøy and Askøy. Dead ahead can be seen the industrial centre of *Salhus*. There are many **Salhus** places bearing this name (formerly Selahus) along the coast and they were all obliged by Royal command to provide shelter for travellers. This Salhus was the last restingplace before reaching Bergen. *Askøy*, on our right, was once Bergen's kitchen garden. Nurserymen and farmers provided — and to some extent still supply — the town with vegetables. Here, too, citizens have built their little summer cottage and huts, which are scattered all over the island.

Bergen greets us on our return with the sight of the "skyscrapers" **Bergen** at Eidsvågneset. The familiar view of Edvard Grieg's native town, encircled by towering mountains, reminds us that our voyage on the coastal express has reached journey's end.

We're back in Bergen at the end of our 2,500-mile voyage. Hope to see you again!